Through the year with
WORDS OF ENCOURAGEMENT

Compiled by Daniel P. Cronin

Foreword by
Cardinal Cahal Daly

St Paul Publications

St Paul Publications
Middlegreen, Slough SL3 6BT, United Kingdom
Moyglare Road, Maynooth, Co. Kildare, Ireland

© St Paul Publications 1992

ISBN 085439 422 2

Printed by The Guernsey Press Co Ltd, Guernsey, C.I.

St Paul Publications is an activity of the priests and brothers of
the Society of St Paul who proclaim the Gospel through the media
of social communication

Contents

Dedicated to
the Society of St Vincent de Paul

Foreword

All of us, no matter what our age and background may be, need to maintain a daily contact with God. You may already be familiar with the suggested practice contained in Father Daniel Cronin's previous books. Now I can commend another of those books to you.

Father Cronin has yet again assembled an extremely varied and balanced collection of sayings and of extracts from the written works of men and women of all times and of many cultures and places. In the first pages alone I have noted the names of St Clement of Rome (third successor of St Peter), Cardinal Newman, Archbishop Romero, Martin Luther King, Louis Pasteur and Nicolas Berdyaev.

A quotation is allotted to each day of the year according to a system of themes. It can be stimulating and thought provoking to read, say a contemporary English nun's view about holiness and then to set that beside a fifteenth century Flemish monk's prayer and the words of living lay people, a man and a woman.

In our world, with its beauty and attractions, there is much pain and suffering (sometimes, sadly, caused by our fellow human beings). The following pages contain eloquent words of encouragement from many people in different circumstances. I hope that you will find much to delight you in this book, and that its use will enable you to bear your burden more hopefully, trustingly and prayerfully.

+ *Cahal Cardinal Daly*
Archbishop of Armagh

Introduction

This book concludes the trilogy; its predecessors being *Words of Wisdom* and *Words of Comfort.* The form of each book has been consistent, to be used in whatever way each reader finds to be helpful. There are no set rules about its use; just allow the Holy Spirit to speak to you through those passages which become your favourites.

I would like to think that every entry chosen for *Words of Encouragement* can justify its inclusion. Clearly not everything will appeal to everyone. Sometimes I have chosen an item because I knew it would help a mother who is going through a very trying patch with her teenage children, others I will have selected especially for busy people who are overwhelmed and discouraged, yet other pieces will have been included for my fellow priests to renew their enthusiasm and pride in the priesthood. I am sure that many are present for reasons I cannot fully articulate, since I am increasingly convinced that the Holy Spirit is particularly active through the channel of any anthologist who abandons him or herself to the divine promptings which most surely come. It may be that God wants to speak directly to you in those passages.

Why focus on 'encouragement'? I have always liked the invitation contained in this passage from the Scriptures:

> Paul and his friends went by sea ... and reached Antioch in Pisidia. Here they went to the synagogue on the sabbath and took their seats. After the lessons from the Law and the Prophets had been read, the presidents of the synagogue sent them a message: 'Brothers, if you would like to address some WORDS OF ENCOURAGEMENT to the congregation, please do so.
>
> Acts of the Apostles, 13:13-15

The need for each of us to be encouraged is a perennial one. Every generation is prone to discouragement and our own is definitely no exception to that. Hence it has been a great pleasure, perhaps even somewhat self-indulgent, to bring together encouraging thoughts and prayers, one for each day of the year.

In choosing quotations for inclusion, I was strongly aware of the need for authenticity. You also have probably found that those who encourage us most when we are facing some difficulty or problem, are those who have experienced and gone through something similar in their own lives. They can speak from the heart and not merely from the intellect. So, there are many quotations relating to Jesus Christ, who went through death and rose to a new life for us. Striking in its own special way is Terry Waite's act of faith, given after his release from captivity. It shows that we often have to be prepared to live a somewhat tedious kind of life. What transforms that is faith, coupled with love – and you will find in this book many quotations about love and attributes of it.

In his prayer (cf. 15 May) John Baillie includes an intention for those of us who write what others will read. I would like to take that one step further and assure you of a place in my prayers, for as long as any need may persist in your lives. I pray that this book will help you to be of good heart, sustained by God's protective arm around you and all whom you love.

I am much indebted to Jane Milward who has assisted me in the research for this book and in proof-reading it; without her help *Words of Encouragement* would not have met the publisher's deadline.

Fr Daniel Cronin

January

1 | Abandonment

Almighty God, Father of our Lord Jesus Christ, grant, we pray, that we might be grounded and settled in your truth by the coming of your Holy Spirit into our hearts.

What we do not know,
    reveal to us;

What is lacking within us,
    make complete;

That which we do know,
    confirm in us;

And keep us blameless in your service,
    through Jesus Christ our Lord.

St Clement of Rome fl. c. 96

2 | Abandonment

God may well do great things in us – he almost certainly will – but for our part it is simply a matter of handing ourselves over to him.

Delia Smith

3 | Abandonment

Father, give to thy child that which he himself knows not how to ask. I dare not ask either for crosses or consolation; I simply present myself before thee, I open my heart to thee. Behold my needs which I know not myself; see and do according to thy tender mercy. Smite or heal, depress or raise me up.

I adore all thy purposes without knowing them.

I am silent; I offer myself in sacrifice.

I yield myself to thee. I would have no other desire than to accomplish thy will.

Teach me to pray.

Pray thyself in me. Amen.

François Fénelon 1651 – 1715

4 Achievement

Four steps to achievement:
plan purposefully,
prepare prayerfully,
proceed positively,
pursue persistently.

William A. Ward 1893 – 19?

5 Action

Nothing would be done at all
if a man waited till
he could do it so well
that no one could find fault with it.

Cardinal John Henry Newman 1801 – 1890

6 Adversity

God is able to give us interior resources to confront the trials and difficulties of life. Each of us faces circumstances in life which compel us to carry heavy burdens of sorrow. Adversity assails us with hurricane force. Glowing sunrises are transformed into darkest nights. Our highest hopes are blasted and our noblest dreams are shattered.

Christianity has never overlooked these experiences. They come inevitably... Admitting the weighty problems and staggering disappointments, Christianity affirms that God is able to give us the power to meet them. He is able to give us the power to meet them. He is able to give us the inner equilibrium to stand tall amid the trials and burdens of life. He is able to provide inner peace among outer storms. This inner stability of the man of faith is Christ's chief legacy to his disciples. He offers neither material resources nor a magical formula that exempts us from suffering and persecution, but he brings an imperishable gift: 'Peace I leave with you.' This is that peace which passeth all understanding.

Martin Luther King 1929 – 1968

7 | Availability

It came to me as an arresting thought: 'What God wants of you is not your ability but your availability'. It is not primarily what one man can do for God in any particular situation that counts, but what God can do through one man or woman who is fully available and responsive to him. Paul's words to the Ephesian Christians remind us still that 'By his power within us' he is able to do infinitely more than we ever dare to ask or imagine. Experience proves, often dramatically, that it is not our ability or the lack of it, but our availability to God that is the clue to all effective Christian action whether by individuals or by groups of Christians.

John Sayers

8 | Availability

I used to ask God to help me,
Then I asked if I might help him,
I ended asking him to do his work through me.

Anon.

9 Baptism

If some day they take the radio station
    away from us,
if they close down our newspaper,
if they don't let us speak,
if they kill all our priests and the bishop too,
and you are left, a people without priests,
each one of you must be God's microphone,
each one of you must be a messenger,
    a prophet.
The Church will always exist
as long as there is one baptized person.
And that one baptized person who is left
    in the world
is responsible before the world for holding aloft
the banner of the Lord's truth
and of his divine justice.

Archbishop Oscar Romero 1917 – 1980

10 Belief

Lord, I believe; help my unbelief
For I believe in your deep love and mercy,
In your forgiving understanding
Of the human heart.
Through lonely watches of the spirit's night
Within the narrow tunnel of my grief,
I know a quiet dawn will come.
Tortured alone in the creeping loathsome dark
And dragged along a labyrinthic maze,
I still believe your healing sun
Will bring the birth of some new day
To break the iron gates of pain,
To bring again life where hopes, broken, lie
Crippled among her ancient battlements;

Lord, I believe that there will surely be
Light, after the midnight burns to death.

Randle Manwaring

11 | Belief

I believe, O God of all gods,
That Thou art the eternal Father of life;
I believe, O God of all gods,
That Thou art the eternal Father of love.

I believe, O Lord and God of the peoples,
That Thou art the creator of the high heavens,
That Thou art the creator of the skies above,
That Thou art the creator of the oceans below.

I believe, O Lord and God of the peoples,
That Thou art He who created my soul and set its
    warp,
Who created my body from dust and from ashes,
Who gave to my body breath, and to my soul its
    possession.

I am giving Thee worship with my whole life,
I am giving Thee assent with my whole power,
I am giving Thee praise with my whole tongue,
I am giving Thee honour with my whole utterance,
I am giving Thee reverence with my whole
    understanding,
I am giving Thee offering with my whole thought,
I am giving Thee praise with my whole fervour,
I am giving Thee humility in the blood of the Lamb.

I am giving Thee love with my whole devotion,
I am giving Thee kneeling with my whole desire,
I am giving Thee love with my whole heart,
I am giving Thee affection with my whole sense;

I am giving Thee my whole existence with my whole
  mind,
I am giving Thee my soul, O God of all gods.

Old Celtic Prayer

12 | Bereavement

Lord in my grief, you comforted me;
Lord in my deep distress, you sustained me;
Lord in my prayerfulness, you listened to me;
Lord in my searching, you led me;
Lord in my dreadful despair, you talked to me;
Lord in my loneliness, you befriended me;
Lord in my anguish, you gave me Peace;
Lord thank you for your Presence,
Lord thank you for your mercy,
Lord thank you for teaching me your ways,
Lord thank you, for being my Friend.

Frances M. Brown

13 | Bereavement

In bereavement we all know that at first memories of
happiness shared bring the tears more than almost
anything else. A photograph of somewhere we spent
that wonderful day, the flowers we planted together,
the music we loved to listen to, all break our hearts. But
after a time we can bear to think of these things, and it
is good to remember how much happiness there was.
Sometimes, indeed, it is only after the other has gone
that we realise how much there was. At the time we
used to fuss and grumble so, that we hardly noticed the
deep inner contentment we shared with them. There is
a lesson here: Remember the good things. Remember
them as they happen day by day. Be grateful for them as

they go by. Then later on they will be a strength and consolation. It is because we remember the 'pastures green' and the 'quiet waters' that we are aware of God's rod and staff comforting us even in the darkest valley.

John Austin Baker

14 Bereavement

Those we love don't go away
    They walk beside us every day
        Unseen – unheard but always near
        Still loved, still missed,
          Still very dear.

15 Bereavement

The comfort of friends in a bereavement

For the kindly thought you had
In offering your sympathy in our loss
For approaching us, and by just being there
It helped, even a little, to ease this cross.

Even the offer of a shoulder to cry on
Is a consolation in times of sorrow and grief
Or the heartfelt sympathy in your handclasp
Can bring a measure of warm gratitude and relief.

Perhaps your sympathy was wordless
And only showed in your eyes
Because you too know the grief that is felt
    When a loved one dies.

Eilís Ní Fheich

16 | Brokenness

Our brokenness is the wound
through which the full power of God
can penetrate our being
and transfigure us in him.

Loneliness is not something from which we must flee
but the place from where we can cry out to God,
where he will find us and we can find him.

Yes, through our wounds
the power of God can penetrate us
and become like rivers of living water
to irrigate the arid earth within us.
Thus we may irrigate the arid earth of others,
so that hope and love are reborn...

> We are a wounded people;
> we can love each other, forgive each other
>   and celebrate together our oneness.

Perhaps we can only truly accept this humiliation
if we live an experience similar to the one
lived by the prodigal son.
If we discover that we are loved and forgiven
    and accepted by the Father
    just as we are,
    in all our brokenness,
    with all the darkness and pain inside us,
then we too can weep in the arms of God,
rejoicing in his forgiveness.

Yes, the cry and the anguish of the poor
triggers off our own cry and anguish;
we touch our point of pain and helplessness.

But then we discover the new name of God,
the name revealed by Jesus,

of the Spirit, the Holy Spirit;
the Father will send a *Paraclete.*
It is a beautiful name,
meaning literally
'the one who answers the cry or the call',
like a mother
who takes in her arms her weeping child.
She is a paraclete.
The name of God is
'the one who answers the cry'.
.Mercy and misery embrace!
We can only know the incredible mercy and love
   of God
if we accept to descend into our misery
and there cry out to him.
Then he will answer, 'Here I am, Beloved,'
and will enfold us in his arms
with a long embrace.

Jean Vanier

17 | Brokenness

There can be no making without breaking; what has
been formed must be broken before it can be transformed. The breaking is painful, but all breaking and
pain is lost sight of in the accomplishment of the
transformation.

R.E.C. Browne 1906 – 1975

18 | Burdens

Cast your burden on the Lord,
   and he will sustain you;
he will never permit
   the righteous to be moved.

Psalm 55:22

19 | Change

We live in a moment of history where change is so speeded up that we begin to see the present only when it is already disappearing.

R.D. Laing

20 | Change

Personal problems are solved much more easily when we take them one at a time. Once you have solved one problem, the next one seems easier. You always begin by selecting a very small, very specific item in your life that you want to change. The sum of all the small changes makes up a new way of life. It is also important for you to begin by selecting the easiest problem you want to solve or at least to pick one which you think is possible to solve.

Edward E. Ford and Robert L. Zorn

21 | Charter of belief

I believe in the supreme worth of the individual and in his right to life, liberty, and the pursuit of happiness.

I believe that every right implies a responsibility; every opportunity, an obligation; every possession, a duty.

I believe that the law was made for man, not man for the law; that government is the servant of the people, not their master.

I believe in the dignity of labour, whether with head or hand; that the world owes no man a living, but that it owes every man an opportunity to make a living.

I believe that thrift is essential to well-ordered living and that economy is a prime requisite of a sound financial structure, whether in government, business or personal affairs.

I believe that truth and justice are fundamental to an enduring social order.

I believe in the sacredness of a promise, that a man's word should be as good as his bond; that character – not wealth or power or position – is of supreme worth.

I believe that the rendering of useful service is the common duty of mankind and that only in the purifying fire of sacrifice is the dross of selfishness consumed and the greatness of the human soul set free.

I believe in the all-wise and all-loving God, named by whatever name, and that the individual's highest fulfilment, greatest happiness, and widest usefulness are to be found in harmony with his will.

I believe that love is the greatest thing in the world; it alone can overcome hate; right can and will triumph over might.

John D. Rockefeller Jr. 1874 – 1960

22 Choices

Two roads diverged in a yellow wood,
And sorry I could not travel both
And be one traveller, long I stood
And looked down one as far as I could
To where it bent in the undergrowth;

Then took the other, as just as fair,
And having perhaps the better claim,

Because it was grassy and wanted wear;
Though as for that the passing there
Had worn them really about the same,

And both that morning equally lay
In leaves no step had trodden black.
Oh, I kept the first for another day!
Yet knowing how way leads on to way,
I doubted if I should ever come back.

I shall be telling this with a sigh
Somewhere ages and ages hence:
Two roads diverged in a wood, and I –
I took the one less travelled by,
And that has made all the difference.

Robert Frost 1874 – 1963

23 | Choices

We who lived in concentration camps can remember
the men who walked through the huts comforting
others, giving away their last piece of bread. They may
have been few in number, but they offer sufficient proof
that everything can be taken from a man but one thing:
the last of the human freedoms – to choose one's
attitude in any given set of circumstances, to choose
one's own way.

Victor Frankl

24 | Chosen people

The 'chosen people', but chosen for what? Not for
pleasure, surely, not for power. No religion is an acceptance of the present condition or a warrant for terrestrial
happiness. If happiness comes, it is incidental to the

performance of function, or, in more solemn language, of mission; and the human situation, spiritual as well as material, is never so satisfactory that it should not, or cannot, be bettered. The 'choice' of a people means the acceptance by them of a specific vocation; and in this case the nature of the vocation is indicated clearly from the first: it is to practice and exemplify a new way of living.

Leon Roth

25 Christianity

How I would like to engrave this great idea on each one's heart: Christianity is not a collection of truths to be believed, of laws to be obeyed, of prohibitions. That makes it very distasteful. Christianity is a person, one who loved us so much, one who calls for our love. Christianity is Christ.

Archbishop Oscar Romero 1917– 1980

26 Christianity

The hour has struck when, after terrible struggle, after an unprecedented de-Christianisation of the world and its passage through all the results of that process, Christianity will be revealed in its pure form. Then it will be clear what Christianity stands for and what it stands against. Christianity will again become the only and the final refuge of man. And when the purifying process is finished, it will be seen that Christianity stands for man and for humanity, for the value and dignity of personality, for freedom, for social justice, for the brotherhood of men and of nations, for enlightenment, for the creation of a new life. And it will be clear that only Christianity stands for these things... But the true and final renaissance will probably begin in the world only after the elementary, everyday problems of human existence are solved for all peoples and nations, after bitter human need and the economic slavery of man have been finally conquered. Only then may we expect a new and more powerful revelation of the Holy Spirit in the world.

Nicolas Berdyaev 1874 – 1948

27 Christianity

I am convinced that the reason why people do not follow Our Lord is not because they cannot believe the Christian faith, but because they are not prepared to let go of other things. They still think that Christianity is about 'thou shalt not.' What a wrong idea! The Christ I follow never spoils life, fun and laughter. He always enriches life with his fullness, fragrance and presence.

Archbishop George Carey

28 Christ-like

It is almost a truism to say that each one of us is fashioned and formed by a hundred hands and more. All the time God has been at work, the potter shaping the clay in accordance with the special design he has always had in his divine mind. That design is Christ, and it is the image and likeness of him that the divine potter is trying to form and express in each one of us.

Cardinal Basil Hume OSB

29 Church

The Church is Catholic because she is throughout the whole world, from one end of the earth to the other;

and because she teaches universally and without fail all
the doctrines which ought to be brought to the knowledge of men concerning things visible and invisible in
earth and heaven; and because she brings to the faith
the whole of mankind, rulers and their subjects, educated and uneducated alike; and because she is a
universal physician and healer of every kind, sins of
soul or of body, and possesses in herself every form of
excellence that can be named, in deeds and words, and
in spiritual gifts of every kind.

St Cyril of Jerusalem c. 315 – 386

30 | Church

The Church is not made up of people who are better
than the rest, but of people who want to become better
than they are.

Anon.

31 | Church

O Saviour, give your heavenly aid
to your Church;
She acknowledges you, she glorifies you,
she recognises no other God
or deliverer except you,
who laid down your life for her.

Accept the supplications of your people,
O Virgin Mother of God,
and intercede unceasingly with your Son,
that we who praise you may be freed
from peril and temptation.
You are, in truth, our ambassadress
and our hope.

St Andrew of Crete c. 660 – 740

February

1 | Church

To his Bride, the Church, Christ left his own robe, a many-coloured robe, woven from top to bottom. It is many-coloured because of the many different Orders, distinguished within it. It is seamless because of the undivided unity of a love that cannot be torn apart, as it is written: 'Who shall separate us from the love of Christ?'

Therefore let there be no division within the Church. Let it remain whole and entire according to its inherited right. Concerning the Church it has been written: 'At your right hand stands the queen in a golden robe, embroidered with varying patterns.'

This is why different people receive different gifts. One person is allotted one kind of gift, one another, irrespective of whether they be a Cistercian or a Cluniac, a Regular or one of the laity. This applies to every Order and to all languages, to both sexes, to every age and condition of life, everywhere and always, from the first person down to the last.

St Bernard of Clairvaux 1090 – 1153

2 | Church

The spiritual life of the Christian Church is not a set of duets: it is a great symphony, in which every person has a part, and no person is independent of the rest.

Evelyn Underhill 1875 – 1941

3 | Church

The core of Jesus' message is the proclamation of the kingdom which is coming and is rendered present in Jesus himself. Though it is not a reality detachable from the Church it transcends the Church's visible bounds. For it is found in a certain way wherever God is ruling through his grace and love: wherever he is overcoming sin and helping human beings to grow toward the great communion offered them in Christ. This activity of God is also found in the hearts of human beings who live outside the perceptible sphere of the Church. But that definitely does not mean that membership of the Church is a matter of indifference. Thus the Church received the mission to announce and establish the kingdom among all peoples. The Church is its sign. In the Church we find the visible manifestation of the project that God is silently carrying out throughout the world. The Church is the place where we find the maximum concentration of the Father's activity. Through the power of the Spirit of Love, the Father is solicitously seeking out human beings to share his own Trinitarian life with them – a gesture of ineffable tenderness. The Church is also the instrument that ushers in the kingdom among human beings in order to spur them on to their definitive goal.

Latin American Bishops' Conference

4 | Comfort

O God, make me brave.
Let me strengthen after pain,
As a tree strengthens after
 rain
Shining and lovely again;
As the blown grass lifts, let
 me rise

From sorrow with quiet eyes,
Knowing Thy way is wise.
God, make me braver.
Life brings such blinding
    things!
Help me to keep Thee in sight,
Knowing all thro' my night,
That out of dark comes light.

5 | Commitment

You must give all or nothing when God asks it. If you have not the courage to give, at least let him take.

François Fénelon 1651 – 1715

6 | Companions

No human being can fully enter the life of others or live it for them. Yet this need not prevent us asking what it might mean to be a *companion* of another on life's journey (and to have others as companions on ours). A companion does not necessarily know the way any better than we do.

Alastair V. Campbell

7 | Compassion

But we cannot just go out and try to practise this kind of
compassion. First we must learn how not to make a
nuisance of ourselves. If we can make friends with
ourselves, if we are willing to be what we are, without
hating parts of ourselves and trying to hide them, then
we can begin to open to others. And if we can begin to
open, without always having to protect ourselves, then
perhaps we can begin to really help others.

Chogyam Trungpa

8 | Confidence

Jesus says to us, in effect: Accept yourself as God
accepts you; be yourself, love yourself properly. Take
off your dark-coloured glasses and see yourself not as
superior or inferior to anyone else, but as you, a person
who matters. You were not meant to go through life on
your hands and knees, you were meant to walk tall.
You are more significant, stronger, wiser and more
creative than you think. I am with you to help you, and
to give you life to the full.

W. Scott McPheat

9 | Confidence

This too will pass away

If I can endure for this minute
Whatever is happening to me
No matter how heavy my heart is
Or how dark the moment may be
If I can remain calm and quiet

With all my world crashing about me
Secure in the knowledge God loves me
When everyone else seems to doubt me
If I can but keep on believing
What I know in my heart to be true
That darkness will fade with the morning
And that this will pass away too
Then nothing in life can defeat me
For as long as this knowledge remains
I can suffer whatever is happening
For I know God will break all the chains
That are binding me tight in the darkness
And trying to fill me with fear
For there is no night without dawning
And I know that my morning is near.

10 | Confidence

Up to now the Lord has helped me wonderfully. I am not yet scared and not yet beaten. The hour of human weakness will no doubt come and sometimes I am depressed when I think of all the things I hoped to do. But I am now a man internally free and far more genuine than I was before. Only now have I sufficient insight to see the thing as a whole...

But one thing is gradually becoming clear – I must surrender myself completely. This is seed time, not harvest. God sows the seed and some time or other he will do the reaping. The one thing I must do is to make sure the seed falls on fertile ground. And I must arm myself against the pain and depression that sometimes almost defeat me. If this is the way God has chosen – and everything indicates that it is – then I must willingly and without rancour make it my way. May others at some future time find it possible to have a better and happier life because we died in this hour of trial. I ask my friends not to mourn, but to pray for me and help me as long as I have need of help. And to be quite clear in their own minds that I was sacrificed, not conquered.

Nor must I forget those to whom I owe so much. May those I have hurt forgive me – I am sorry for having injured them. May those to whom I have been untrue forgive me – and I am sorry for having failed them. May those to whom I have been proud and overbearing forgive me – I repent my arrogance. And may those to whom I have been unloving forgive me – I repent my hardness. Oh yes – long hours spent in this cell with fettered wrists and my body and spirit tormented must have broken down a great deal that was hard in me. Much that was unworthy and worthless has been committed to the flames…

And so to conclude I will do what I so often did with my fettered hands and what I will gladly do again and again as long as I have breath left – I will give my blessing. I will bless this land and the people; I will bless the Church and pray that her fountains may flow again fresher and more freely; I will bless all those who have believed in me and trusted me, all those I have wronged and all those who have been good to me – too good.

Alfred Delp 1907 – 1945

1 Contentment

Those who want much, are always much in need;
   happy the man to whom God gives with a sparing
      hand
    what is sufficient for his wants.

Quintus Horace 65 – 8 BC

12 Conversion

It is difficult to endure conversion because it seems to put into jeopardy our very lifestyle and ministry, but even more so because we sense that it touches the very roots of our life. It reaches deep into our being – our personality, our choices, our very self. It touches in places that are unknown, places where we are strangers. To begin a journey into an unfamiliar, haunting land is frightening, but not to know whether we will find life or death, blessing or curse, at the end can be terrifying. To enter the journey with all its uncertainties proves the possibility of finding life and life in abundance. Not to begin the journey, but to harden and to steel oneself against it, is already death.

Paul Robb SJ

13 Conversion

A sense of homecoming, of picking up the threads of a lost life, of responding to a bell that had long been ringing, of taking a place at a table that had long been vacant.

Malcolm Muggeridge 1903 – 1990

14 Courage

God gives me courage in proportion to my sufferings. I feel at this moment I couldn't suffer any more, but I'm not afraid, since if they increase, he will increase my courage at the same time.

St Thérèse of Lisieux 1873 – 1897

15 | Crucifix

I look at Your Hands – so hurt – so torn
I look at Your Head – so pierced with thorn
I look at Your Body – hanging there
And I cry 'Forgive me Lord – I care.'

I look at my life – so full of wrong
I look at Your Heart – where I belong
I look at Your Love – still shining through
And in sorrow shed a tear for You.

I look at the Cross on Easter Day
I look at the price You had to pay.
I offer my life in silent prayer
To thank You, Lord, for being there.

Connie Ford

16 | Death

Merciful Father, be with us as we gather in this house, the home of our dear one who has gone forward to life everlasting. We remember all her goodness. May her memory be a blessing.

Help us to remember that the soul does not die, and our dear one has gone to that eternal home which you prepared for us when our work on earth is done, and our time here has ended. Open the gates of mercy for her. May she enter into everlasting peace. In your light we see beyond the frontiers of death to the life that has no end.

This house was built by human hands, but we shall come together in a home where we shall never part, surrounded by your presence. Amen.

17 Death

It has always seemed to me a major tragedy that so many people go through life haunted by the fear of death – only to find when it comes that it's as natural as life itself. For very few are afraid to die when they get to the very end. In all my experience only one seemed to feel any terror – a woman who had done her sister a wrong which it was too late to right.

Something strange and beautiful happens to men and women when they come to the end of the road. All fear, all horror disappears. I have often watched a look of happy wonder dawn in their eyes when they realised this was true. It is all part of the goodness of nature and, I believe, of the illimitable goodness of God.

An experienced nurse

18 Death

When we are dead, and people weep for us and grieve, let it be because we touched their lives with beauty and simplicity. Let it not be said that life was good to us, but, rather, that we were good to life.

Jacob P. Rudin

19 Defeat

We never get over the wounds we have received; our defeats are always defeats. However, if we allow ourselves to become completely absorbed in our own misfortune, if we cut ourselves off, then the defeat creates a crippling selfishness and is death-dealing indeed. But if we resist the whirlpool of selfishness and turn outwards, determined to show care and generosity and love where it is needed, if we keep our hearts open, then the transforming change can and will take place.

Roderick Strange

20 | Desire

The whole life of a good Christian is a holy desire. What you desire you cannot see yet. But the desire gives you the capacity, so that when it does happen that you see, you may be fulfilled.

St Augustine 354 – 430

21 | Desire

You must want like God that you may be satisfied like God. Were you not made in his image? There is nothing wrong with wanting as such. Our wants, our desires, our loves lead us, if rightly ordered, to God himself. It is a disorder of desire that leads men away from God. When we dote upon the perfections and beauties of some one creature, we do not love that too much, but other things too little. Never was anything in this world loved too much, but many things have been loved in a false way, and all in too short a measure.

Thomas Traherne c. 1636 – 1674

22 | Difficulties

I pray today for people faced with difficult decisions: decisions which will seriously affect their lives and the lives of their loved ones: decisions about jobs, about their marriage, about where to live, about money.

I pray for those who can see no way through their problems: for whom it is all too much.

Help them to see that you, who control the universe, are in control of their lives too.

Further Everyday Prayers

23 | Discipleship

There are times when I can visualise Our Lord at the break of day standing by my bed and saying: 'Get up, follow me.' Whether I am conscious of it or not, in effect that invitation, that loving but insistent command, is given to me every day. Each new morning is the opportunity to start again. Yesterday there may have been inadequacies and failures but today Christ renews his call: 'Follow me. I have chosen you. I need you.' Who can fail to respond to the thought that God needs our willing collaboration?

Cardinal Basil Hume OSB

24 | Discouragement

Should we feel at times disheartened and discouraged, a confiding thought, a simple movement of the heart towards God will renew our powers. Whatever he may demand of us, he will give us at that moment the strength and the courage that we need.

François Fénelon 1651 – 1715

25 | Dying

It seems necessary, unless the dying person is in a coma or cannot communicate, that he should be told he is dying. It may be difficult to actually take such a step, but if one is a friend or a husband or wife, then this is the greatest opportunity of communicating trust. It is a delightful situation, that at last somebody really cares about you, somebody who is not playing a game of hypocrisy, is not going to tell you a lie in order to please you, which is what has been happening throughout your whole life. This comes down to the ultimate truth, it is fundamental trust, which is extremely beautiful. We should really try to generate that principle.

Actually relating with the dying person is very important, telling him that death is not a myth at that point, but that it is actually happening. 'It is actually happening, but we are your friends, therefore we are watching your death. We know that you are dying and you know that you are dying, we are really meeting together at this point.' That is the finest and best demonstration of friendship and communication, it presents tremendously rich inspiration to the dying person.

Chogyam Trungpa

26 | Easter

The Lord is risen!
He is risen indeed!
Alleluia!

Lord Jesus, we greet you, risen from the dead.

We thought that your way of love was a dead end,
    leading only to the cross: now we see that it is the
    way to life.

We thought that your whole life was wasted: now we
   know that it was gloriously worthwhile.
We thought that your suffering was pointless: now we
   can see God's purpose in it.
We thought that death was the end of us: now we
   know that your life was too great to be ended by
   death.

Lord Jesus, we greet you, risen from the dead.

Contemporary Prayers for Public Worship

27 | Empathy

When someone is desperately asking us to help them
deny the reality of their pain, it requires strength to stay
silent. Yet silence is often our greatest service. By
remaining *with* people, but at the same time refusing to
take the escape from pain they seek, we can restore
their courage to voice their deepest fears and express
the anguish they find so threatening. Our main task is to
wait and watch with them, that simple service which
Jesus asked for (in vain) from his friends.

Alastair V. Campbell

28 | Encouragement

Your way through life
will not remain the same.
There are years of happiness and
years of suffering.
There are years of abundance
and years of poverty,
years of hope and disappointment,
of building up, and of breaking down.

But God has a firm hold on you
through everything.

There are years of strength
and years of weakness,
years of uncertainty, years of doubt.
It is all part of life,
and it is worth the effort
to live it to the end
and not give up before it is accomplished.

You need never stop growing,
a new future is always possible.
Even on the other side of death.
A new existence waits for you
in the fullness of that glory
which God has prepared for you
from the beginning.

29
LEAP
YEAR

Encouragement

Help me at all times, O God,
    to encourage and not to dishearten,
    to be more ready to praise than to condemn,
    to uplift rather than to disparage,
    to hide rather than to expose the faults of others.
O risen and exalted Christ, dwell in me,
    that I may live with the light of hope in my eyes,
    the Word of life on my lips,
    and your love in my heart.
Help me, O Holy Spirit, to seek you faithfully,
    to hold you steadfastly,
    to show you unfailingly,
    for Christ's sake.

T. Glyn Thomas 1905 – 1973

March

1 | End of the world

The world will end in joy, because it is a place of
sorrow.
When joy has come, the purpose of the world has
gone.
The world will end in peace, because it is a place of
war.
When peace has come, what is the purpose of the
world?
The world will end in laughter, because it is a place of
tears.
Where there is laughter, who can longer weep?
And only complete forgiveness brings all this to bless
the world.
In blessing it departs, for it will not end as it began.

Gerald Jampolsky

2 | Eternal life

This is eternal life;
a life of everlasting love,
showing itself in everlasting good works;
and whosoever lives that life,
he lives the life of God,
and hath eternal life.

Charles Kingsley 1819– 1875

3 | Eternal life

All that you have experienced is of value, is important,
is serious – so serious that God preserves it and gathers
it together. And one day he will say to you: 'You have
not just lived your life in the past, but you will live it

always. It will be yours, you will take it up again in the eternal light of the beyond, but with a quite different clarity, quite a different density."

Henri Boulad SJ

4 | Eucharist

A prayer inspired by the Mass

O Lord!
Look into our hearts this day and read us
Look into our souls this day and hear us
When we thrust out our hands for help – hold us
When we open our arms for love – embrace us
When we raise our eyes heavenward – speak to us
When we bow our heads to thee – bless us
When we give of ourselves – come to us. Amen

Judith Ann Pounder

5 | Eucharist

Was ever another command so obeyed? For century after century, spreading slowly to every continent and country and among every race on earth, this action has been done, in every conceivable human circumstance. Men have found no better thing than this to do for kings at their crowning and for criminals going to the scaffold; for armies in triumph or for a bride and bridegroom in a little country church; for the wisdom of the Parliament of a mighty nation or for a sick old woman afraid to die; for a schoolboy sitting an examination or for Columbus setting out to discover America; in thankfulness because my father did not die of pneumonia... tremulously, by an old monk on the fiftieth anniversary of his vows; furtively, by an exiled bishop who had hewn timber all day in a prison camp near Murmansk; gorgeously, for the canonisation of St Joan of Arc – one could fill many pages with the reasons why men have done this, and not tell a hundredth part of them. And best of all, week by week and month by month, on a hundred thousand successive Sundays, faithfully, unfailingly, across all the parishes of Christendom, the pastors have done this just to make holy the people of God.

Dom Gregory Dix 1901 – 1952

6 Experience

Upon the wreckage of thy yesterday
Design the structure of tomorrow;
Lay strong cornerstones with strength and purpose;
Great blocks of wisdom from past despair;
Strong mighty pillars resolve to set
Deep in tear-wet mortar of regret,
Work well with patience, tho' thy toil be slow,
Yet day by day thine edifice shall grow.
Believe in God and in thine own self believe,
Then all thou hast desired, thou shalt achieve.

Ella Wheeler Wilcox 1855 – 1919

7 Faith

Perhaps this is the real message of faith for the world now: the heart of man can change at any moment, every instant has eternal value because in any moment of your life you might find the courage to open the door to Christ.

This is what happened to me.

Marco Barbone

8 | Faith

Faith is the light of time, it alone recognises truth without seeing it, touches what it cannot feel, looks upon this world as though it did not exist, sees what is not apparent. It is the key to celestial treasures, the key to the unfathomable mystery and knowledge of God. Faith conquers all the fantasy of falsehood; through faith God reveals and manifests himself, defying all things. Faith removes the veil and uncovers eternal truth. When souls are given the understanding of faith, God speaks to them through all creation, and the universe becomes for them a living testimony which the finger of God continually traces before their eyes, the record of every passing moment, a sacred scripture. The sacred books which the Holy Spirit has dictated are only the beginnings of divine guidance for us. Everything that happens is a continuation of the scriptures, expounding for us what has not been written. Faith explains the one through the other. It is an abstraction presenting the vast extent of divine action summarised in the scriptures, in which souls can discover the key to all its mysteries... Faith is only living at its best when sensible appearances contradict and attempt to destroy it... To find God is good in the trivial and most ordinary events as in the greatest, is to have not an ordinary, but a great and extraordinary faith... How delightful the peace one enjoys when one has learned by faith to see God in this way through all creatures as through a transparent veil. Darkness become light and bitterness sweet... There is nothing that faith does not penetrate and seek out. It passes beyond darkness, and no matter how deep the shadows, it passes through them to the truth which it always finally embraces, and from which it is never separated.

Jean-Pierre de Caussade 1675 – 1751

9 | Faith

God's silence is the boundless sphere where alone our love can produce its act of faith in his love. If in our earthly life his love had become so manifest to us that we would know beyond a shadow of a doubt what we really are, namely God's own beloved, then how could we prove to him the daring courage and fidelity of our love? How could such a fidelity exist at all? How could our love, in the ecstasy of faith, reach out beyond this world into his world and into his heart? He has veiled his love in the stillness of his silence so that our love might reveal itself in faith.

Karl Rahner SJ 1904 – 1984

10 | Faith

'The remarkable thing about faith is that it isn't a sudden flash from heaven or a sudden insight of that kind. It is just something that quietly sustains. I would say to myself: "You can do your worst but you can't destroy me, never." They didn't.'

Terry Waite – in a BBC interview
on his release from captivity

11 | Fallibility

... to know that one is fallible under God is very different from just being a muddled human being. If at times we feel we are groping in the dark and being given responsibilities too great for us, we can also know that the God who sees and knows us in our weakness, forgives and restores us in his love. It thus becomes possible to make the decisions which have to be made, without complacency and without constant anxiety, because the God who gives us his law on Sinai, is also the God of love and forgiveness who has visited and redeemed his people.

Archbishop John Habgood

12 | Farewell

There will come a time when my links with earth will grow weaker, when my powers fail, when I must bid farewell to dear ones still rooted in this life with their tasks to fulfil and their loved ones to care for, when I must detach myself from the loveliest things and begin the lonely journey. Then I shall hear the voice of my beloved Christ, saying 'It is I, be not afraid.' So with my hand in his, from the dark valley I shall see the shining City of God and climb with trusting steps and be met by the Father of souls and clasped in the everlasting arms.

George Appleton

13 | Fear

Only confidence in God is capable of giving me wings; fear, by contrast, freezes me and paralyses my being.

Sister Consolata 1903 – 1946

14 | Fear

The Lord is my light and my salvation;
   whom shall I fear?
The Lord is the stronghold of my life;
   of whom shall I be afraid?

Psalm 27:1

15 | Fidelity

Our Lord and reason do not demand results in the things we do, but only our faithful and whole-hearted co-operation, endeavour and diligence; for these do depend on us, whereas success does not.

St Francis de Sales 1567 – 1622

16 | Forgiveness

Give us grace, dear Lord, to receive forgiveness from others when we have wronged them. Take away our pride and resentment and give us the humility and courage to accept fully and freely the forgiveness that they offer to us – for Jesus' sake.

I offer also for all those whom I have in any way grieved, vexed, oppressed and scandalised, by word or deed, knowingly or unknowingly: that thou mayest equally forgive us all our sins, and all our offences against each other.

St Thomas More 1478 – 1535

17 | Forgiveness

I am so certain of the guidance of God's hand that I hope to be maintained always in this certainty. You must never doubt that I walk thankfully and joyfully this path in which I am being led. My life in the past has been filled to overflowing with God's goodness, and above guilt stands the forgiving love of him who was crucified. I am most thankful of all for the people whom I have known, and hope only that they will never have to sorrow over me, and that they too will gratefully always be certain only of the kindness and forgiveness of God.

Dietrich Bonhoeffer 1906 – 1945
from a letter dated 23 August 1944

18 | Forgiveness

We prayed so that all bitterness could be taken from us and we could start the life for our people again without hatred. We knew out of our own suffering that life cannot begin for the better except by us all forgiving one another. For if one does not forgive, one does not understand; and if one does not understand, one is afraid; and if one is afraid, one hates; and if one hates, one cannot love. And no new beginning on earth is possible without love, particularly in a world where men increasingly not only do not know how to love but cannot even recognise it when it comes searching for them. The first step towards this love then must be forgiveness.

Sir Laurens van der Post
Written about a group of people who had
survived a massacre in South Africa

19 | Forgiveness

Forgive me my sins, O Lord;
forgive me the sins of my youth
and the sins of mine age,
the sins of my soul and sins of my body,
my secret and my whispering sins,
the sins I have done to please myself
and the sins I have done to please others.
Forgive those sins which I know,
and the sins which I know not;
forgive them, O Lord, forgive them all
of thy great goodness. Amen.

Anon.

20 | Forgiveness

One further point about confession: the sharing with another human being of our weaknesses, trials, temptations and sins can be a very healing experience. It can be a great relief to free the bottled up guilt and get it off one's chest. For me personally it is a source of peace that there is no conscious area of my past, however shameful or dark or humiliating, that I have not shared with a confessor. And the humbling of ourselves which such sharing requires is part of the healing process. Furthermore, a wise confessor is able, with the help of the Holy Spirit, to discern our needs and give wise advice. The wise counselling is normally a necessary part of the process of inner healing which we all need.

All this emphasises the need for the confessor and the penitent to pray seriously to the Holy Spirit for light, love and healing before the confession. We should expect the Holy Spirit to come with power when this sacrament is celebrated – even though we may not always feel the power. We shall see more of this power and healing as we pray more truly: 'Come, Holy Spirit.'

Dom Benedict Heron OSB

21 | Frailty

And when we have fallen, through frailty or blindness, then our courteous Lord touches us, stirs and calls us. And then he wills that we should see our wretchedness and humbly acknowledge it. But it is not his will that we should stay like this, nor does he will that we should busy ourselves too much with self-accusation; nor is it his will that we should despise ourselves. But he wills that we should quickly turn to him.

He is quick to clasp us to himself, for we are his joy and his delight, and he is our salvation and our life.

Wonderful and splendid is the place where the Lord lives. And therefore it is his will that we turn quickly at his gracious touch, rejoicing more in the fullness of his love than sorrowing over our frequent failures.

Julian of Norwich c.1342 – after 1413

22 | Friendship

The glory of friendship is not the outstretched hand, nor the kindly smile, nor the joy of companionship; it is the spiritual inspiration that comes to one when he discovers that someone else believes in him and is willing to trust him.

Ralph Waldo Emerson 1803 – 1882

23 | Friendship

A blessed thing it is for any man or woman to have a friend: one human soul whom we can trust utterly; who knows the best and the worst of us; who will speak the honest truth to us, while the world flatters us to our faces and laughs at us behind our backs; who will counsel and reproof in the day of prosperity and self-conceit; but who will comfort and encourage us in the day of difficulty and sorrow when the world leaves us alone to fight our own battles as we can.

If we have had the good fortune to win such a friend, let us do anything rather than lose him. We must give and forgive; live and let live. If our friends have faults we must bear with them. We must hope all things, believe all things, endure all things, rather than lose that most precious of all earthly possessions – a trusty friend. And a friend, once won, need never be lost, if we will only be trusty and true ourselves.

Charles Kingsley 1819 – 1875

24 Friendship

Let there be love and understanding among us;
let peace and friendship be our shelter from life's
    storms.
Eternal God, help us to walk with good companions,
to live with hope in our hearts and eternity in our
    thoughts,
that we may lie down in peace and rise up
to find our hearts waiting to do your will.

Jewish prayer

25 Friendship

If you have a friend worth loving,
    Love him. Yes, and let him know
That you love him, ere life's evening
    Tinges his brow with sunset glow.
Why should good words ne'er be said
    Of a friend till he is dead?

Daniel W. Hoyt 1845 – 1936

26 Future

When Our Lord spoke of the future he gave his disciples no optimistic hopes, no vision of social progress; he described all the things that we are afraid of today and more – wars, persecutions, disasters and the distress of nations. But strange to say he used this forecast of calamity as a motive for hope. 'When you see these things," he said, 'look up and lift up your heads, for your redemption is at hand.' That may seem a strange philosophy of history but it is the authentic philosophy of Christ, and if the prospect of these things causes us to hang down our heads instead of lifting them up, it shows that there is something wrong with our point of view. I know we are apt to feel that this does not apply to us – that it merely refers to the end of the world. But to the Christian the world is always ending, and every historical crisis is, as it were, a rehearsal for the real thing.

Christopher Dawson 1889 – 1970

27 Future

Candles

The days of our future stand before us
like a row of lighted candles –
golden, warm and lively little candles.

The days gone by remain behind us,
a mournful line of burnt-out candles,
the nearest ones are still smoking,
cold candles, melted and bent.

I do not want to look at them – their form saddens me,
and it saddens me to recall their first light.
I look ahead at my lighted candles.

I do not want to look back, lest I see and shudder,
how quietly the sombre line lengthens,
how quickly the burnt-out candles multiply.

C.P. Cavafy

28 | Gentleness

Softness and gentleness may be regarded as 'bad business' and inimical to successful ambition. But they are essential to Christian conduct.

Lord Longford

29 | Gift of life

In dwelling upon the mystery of death and that which follows it... I seize upon the truth which, in the case of this mystery, is always reflected for me in this present life, and I give thanks to him who has conquered death for having put to flight its dark shadows and for having revealed the light. And also before my death, the moment of total and complete severance from this present life, I feel the need to celebrate the gift, the fortune, the beauty, the shape of this fleeting existence itself. Lord, I thank you for having called me into this life, and, all the more, for having made me a Christian, for having granted me rebirth and having destined me for the fullness of life. I feel equally the need to thank and bless those who mediated to me the life you have given me, O Lord: those who brought me into this life (blessings upon my most worthy parents), those who educated me, loved me, helped me, surrounded me with good example, with care, affection, goodness, courtesy, friendship, faithfulness and respect. I think with gratitude of those natural and spiritual relationships which have given birth, help, comfort, and meaning to my humble existence: what gifts, what beautiful and valuable things, what great hope I have received in this world. Now that the day is drawing to a close, now that all is coming to an end and fading from this temporal, earthly scene, so splendid and dramatic, how can I thank you enough, O Lord, after the gift of this natural life for that still higher life of faith and of grace and in which alone that part of me which lives on has its final refuge? How can I celebrate your goodness, O Lord, for having received me into the bosom of the Catholic Church? For having called and ordained me into the priesthood of Christ, for having had the joy and the mission of serving souls, of serving the young, the poor, the people of God, and for having had the honour, which I am not worthy of, of being a minister of the Holy Church, in Rome, and then in Milan as archbishop on the chair of St Ambrose, and finally on the supreme, awesome, and holy chair of St Peter? 'I will sing forever of your mercy, O Lord.' May my greetings and blessing reach all those whom I met in this earthly pilgrimage, those who were my co-workers, my helpers, and my friends – how numerous they were, how good, how generous and how dear.

Pope Paul VI 1879 – 1978
Part of his Last Will and Testament

30 | Giving

The more we give ourselves –
    in genuine love of God and of others –
        the more we become our true selves.

Andrew O'Donohoe

31 | God

We know that in everything God works for good with those who love him, who are called according to his purpose.

Romans 8:28

April

1 God

O Lord,
Love me intensely,
Love me often and long!
For the more you love me, the purer I become.
The more intensely you love me, the more beautiful I
    become.
The longer you love me, the holier I become.

St Mechthild of Magdeburg c. 1210 – c. 1280

2 God

God, who needs nothing, loves into existence wholly
superfluous creatures in order that he may love and
perfect them.

C.S. Lewis 1898 – 1963

3 God

No, I shall never believe in:…
the God who does not allow people to talk familiarly
    to him,
the grandfather-God whom one can twist around one's
    little finger,
the God who makes himself the monopoly of a
    church, a race, a culture or a caste,
the God who doesn't need man,
the judge-God who can give a verdict only with a rule
    book in his hands,
the God incapable of smiling at many of man's
    awkward mistakes,
the God who 'sends' people to hell,
the God who does not know how to hope,
the God who can be fully explained by philosophy,

the God incapable of forgiving what many men
    condemn,
the God incapable of redeeming the wretched,
the God who prevents man from growing, and
    conquering,
the God who demands that if a man is to believe he
    must give up being a man,
the God capable of being accepted and understood by
    those who do not love,
the God who says 'You will pay for that!'
the God who sometimes regrets having given man free
    will,
the God who stifles earthly reform and gives hope
    only for the future life,
the God who puts law before conscience.

Juan Arias

4 | God's action

In the course of my own journey I've observed that usually (God) adapts his light to our eyes.

All said and done, the faith God requires of us is reasonable, simple and straightforward...

Normally the course we run to reach God is the same one God runs to meet us.

The meeting takes place about half-way and the reason for this is a simple one.

God doesn't want to work harder than he needs and wants to train us as children, not as slaves.

Carlo Carretto

5 | God's action

It never occurred to me to question God's doings or lack of doings while I was an inmate of Auschwitz, although of course I understand others did... I was no less or no more religious because of what the Nazis did to us; and I believe my faith in God was not undermined in the least. It never occurred to me to associate the calamity we were experiencing with God, to blame him, or to believe in him less or cease believing in him at all because he didn't come to our aid. God doesn't owe us that, or anything. We owe our lives to him. If someone believes God is responsible for the death of six million because he didn't somehow do something to save them, he's got his thinking reversed. We owe God our lives for the few or many years we live, and we have the duty to worship him and do so as he commands us. That's what we're here on earth for, to be in God's service, to do God's bidding.

Reeve Robert Brenner

6 | God's presence

The light of God surrounds me,
   The love of God enfolds me,
      The power of God protects me,
The presence of God watches over me,
   Wherever I am, God is.

7 | Gospel

Forget about sharing 'ideas', especially 'beautiful ideas', on the Gospel. Concentrate rather on sharing a life transformed by the Gospel.

Michel Quoist

8 | Grace

But God loved us with so much love that he was generous with his mercy: when we were dead through our sins, he brought us to life with Christ – it is through grace that you have been saved – and raised us up with him and gave us a place with him in heaven, in Christ Jesus.

This was to show for all ages to come, through his goodness towards us in Christ Jesus, how infinitely rich he is in grace. Because it is by grace that you have been saved, through faith; not by anything of your own, but by a gift from God; not by anything you have done, so that nobody can claim the credit. We are God's work of art, created in Christ Jesus to live the good life as from the beginning he had meant us to live it.

Ephesians 2:4-10

9 | Gratitude

O God,
    you have given so much to me;
        give me one thing more,
            a grateful heart.

George Herbert 1593 – 1633

10 | Gratitude

To be grateful is to recognise the love of God in everything he has given us – and he has given us everything. Every breath we draw is a gift of his love, every moment of existence is a grace, for it brings with it immense graces from him. Gratitude therefore takes nothing for granted, is never unresponsive, is constantly awakening to new wonder and to praise of the goodness of God. For the grateful man knows that God is good, not by hearsay but by experience. And that is what makes all the difference.

Thomas Merton 1915 – 1968

11 | Gratitude

Many times a day I realise how much my own outer and inner life is built upon the labours of my fellow-men, both living and dead, and how earnestly I must exert myself in order to give in return as much as I have received.

Albert Einstein 1879 – 1955

12 | Growth

There are some precise stages in the growth of the heart.

Tiny children live by love and presence – the time of childhood is a time of trust.

Adolescents live by generosity, utopian ideals and hope.

Adults become realistic, commit themselves and assume responsibilities, this is the time of fidelity.

Finally, old people refind the time of confidence which is also wisdom... they have time to observe, to contemplate and to forgive.

They have a whole sense of the meaning of human life, of acceptance and realism.

They know that living has not just to do with action and running; they know it is also to do with welcome and loving.

Jean Vanier

13 Guidance

Lord, what we have not, give us.
  Lord, what we know not, teach us.
Lord, what we are not, make us.
  Forgive what we have been.
Sanctify what we are
  And order what we shall be,
For your mercy's sake.

14 Guilt

It is useless for men and women to know their guilt unless at the same time and to the same degree they consciously experience the grace and love of Christ which saves them.

Henri Boulad SJ

15 Handicapped

Lord Jesus, when you were hanging on the Cross of Calvary, you were rejected by so many people. It must have hurt you so much because you had given all you had of yourself to others. You had healed their wounds, you had comforted them, you had performed miracles so that man had enough to eat. But still you were rejected by mankind. Jesus, sometimes we are rejected because we are handicapped, we are too slow, we may cause others embarrassment. But it is not our fault, we are your children and made in your own image and likeness.

Lord, you know that when we are rejected, the wound cuts so deeply inside. Every time it happens we think it could not possibly happen again and it can't hurt us any more. Dear Jesus, you know only too well that the more it happens, the more it hurts. You know better than anyone just how deep the wound is. Please, Jesus, help us to turn the other cheek as you did when you hung on the Cross and said: 'Father, forgive them for they know not what they do.'

Very often nothing can take away or make up for the pain of rejection so, Jesus, help us to turn to you in the knowledge and belief that although others may reject us, we know for sure that you are the one person who knows and will accept us as we are. Lord, if our cross has got to be one of rejection, please give us the strength and the courage to take it up and follow you, knowing that this is the only way to enter the Kingdom of Heaven. We know, Lord, that pain and suffering no longer exist when we have entered the Kingdom of Heaven.

Elizabeth Greeley

16 | Happiness

Don't ever sell yourself short. You can change if you make realistic plans and work at them. The paradox of happiness is that you first must give in order to get. Steer clear of negative people who are always critical of everything life has to offer. Use your time and your talents wisely, but use them.

Edward E. Ford and Robert L. Zorn

17 Happiness

The greatest happiness of life is the conviction that we are loved – loved for ourselves, or rather, loved in spite of ourselves.

Victor Hugo 1802 – 1885

18 Heaven

Much on earth is hidden from us, but there is given us in recompense the secret conviction of our living bond with another world, a celestial and loftier world; and the very roots of our thoughts and sensations are not here but there, in other worlds. And that is why philosophers say that on earth it is impossible to know the essence of things.

Feodor Dostoievsky 1821 – 1881

19 Heaven

In heaven we will live and live more fully and satisfy-ingly than ever before. And that life will involve all the really important elements of what we know as life: relationships, development, knowledge, communica-tion... We shall recognise our loved ones but more by who they are than by what they look like. But better than that, we shall know them with a depth and insight and love unimaginable in our present human existence.

David Winter

20 Hell

Hell is total preoccupation with self.
Hell is the condition of being tone deaf

to the word of grace,
blind to the presence of God,
unable to discern his image in another person.
Hell is that state in which we no longer
catch the fragrance of life.
Hell is to live in the presence of love
and not know it, not feel it, not be warmed by it.
It is to live in the Father's house like the older son
  (Luke 15)
but be insensitive to the Father's love.
Hell is to be unaware of God's world,
God's people, the reality of God in oneself;
it is to have the doors in life closed tight,
to abide in one's own darkness.

Robert Raines

21 Holiness

Let us remind ourselves over and over again that holiness has to do with very ordinary things: truthfulness, courtesy, kindness, gentleness, consideration for others, contentment with one's lot, honesty and courage in the face of life, reliability, dutifulness.

Ruth Burrows

22 Holiness

There is no holiness, Lord, if you withdraw your hand.
No wisdom is of any use if you no longer guide it.
No strength can avail if you do not preserve it.
No purity is safe if you do not protect it.
No watchfulness on our part can affect anything
unless your holy vigilance is present with us.
If you abandon us, we sink and perish;
but if you come to us we are raised up and we live.

Thomas à Kempis 1380 – 1471

23 | Holiness

'It is a dreadful thing to fall into the hands of the living God', we are told in the Letter to the Hebrews; though it would be more dreadful to fall out of them. Therefore, in some ways, one feels it would be better never to have any contact with holiness of any kind. Certainly it would be more comfortable because the demands made upon us if we are to acquire knowledge of holiness are terrifying. The trouble is that once you find yourself launched upon the road to holiness there is no turning back, ever. Your best chance really is to make sure that you never actually leave base but seek assurance instead by repeating to yourself that the aspiration towards holiness is a vain illusion: sanctity is an impossible ideal, unattainable by frail human beings. This is a stance which can be maintained so long as you take care never to meet a holy person, whether in the flesh or on film or in a book – but especially in the flesh, because once you have met, say, Mother Teresa you can no longer go on saying that sanctity is all very well in theory but in fact it is impossible. It has been done; therefore it can be done; and excuses are no longer plausible. For this reason, worldly people give holy people a wide berth, keeping their distance from them, knowing in their shrewd, worldly way that holy people are dangerous; they are dynamite.

Donald Nicholl

24 | Holiness

In its history the light of the Church has been kept shining through the lives of individual Christians, who have refused to get bogged down in disputes and quarrels, but who have lived lives of such holiness that their memories are still loved centuries later.

Rosemary Hartill

25 Holy Spirit

The outpouring of his Holy Spirit is really the outpouring of his love, surrounding and penetrating your little soul with a peaceful, joyful delight in his creature: tolerant, peaceful love, full of longsuffering and gentleness, working quietly, able to wait for results, faithful, devoted, without variableness or shadow of turning. Such is the charity of God.

Love breaks down the barrier that shuts most of us from heaven. That thought is too much for us really, yet it is the central truth of the spiritual life. And that loving self-yielding to the Eternal Love – that willingness that God shall possess, indwell, fertilise, bring forth the faith of his Spirit in us, instead of our own – is the secret of all Christian power and Christian peace.

Evelyn Underhill 1875 – 1941

26 Holy Spirit

When we face up to life with all its insecurities and ambiguities, we develop insight on how to deal with them. This is a gift of the Holy Spirit, who is always working in our life situations whether we recognise this or not.

Martin H. Padovani

27 Holy Spirit

All that is true,
  by whomsoever spoken,
    is from the Holy Spirit.

St Ambrose c. 339 – 397

28 | Hope

Hope is knowing that
there is love.
It is trust in tomorrow.
It is falling asleep and waking
again when the sun rises.
In the midst of a gale at sea,
it is to discover land.
In the eyes of another,
it is to see that someone
understands you.
As long as there is still hope
there will also be prayer.
And God will be holding
you in his hands.

29 | Hope

The fact that the Lord is coming is a far more important
issue than questions of when it will all take place, or the
precise nature of the events which will accompany his
coming. He is coming – *that* is the great reality; exactly
when and precisely how, though important in their
way, are in the end secondary issues. Christ is coming,
he is destined to reign in his eternal glory and to inherit
the glory and honour of heaven and earth. That and
nothing else is the substance of the Christian hope, and
that is the centre around which all other aspects of the
Last Things find their proper place.

Bruce Milne

30 | Hope

If you have hope
You have everything.

Without hope
There is nothing...

Oh, Lord, grant me the
Gift of hope.

When reason runs dry
May hope for ever
Burn in me,

Until it be like
A fire,

Never giving up.
Always believing.
Hoping.

Published in the Compassionate Friends *newsletter*

May

1 | Hope

God our Father, we know that your will can never lead us where your grace can not keep us. Be with all who carry heavy crosses this day and send them help in the care of friends, so that the cross of your Son may be for them a signpost to hope. Amen.

John J. McCullagh

2 | Humanity

There is no substitute for the human touch. A materially advanced society may provide a welfare cushion to soften the material suffering of those in economic need; and indeed such a safety net is, we are almost all agreed today, a basic measure of social civilisation. But it cannot provide what is truly wanted: love, friendship, emotional bonds between people, emotional support, the care that comes from personal friendship.

Mary Kenny

3 | Humanity

I do believe that all human beings, unique and different in so many respects, share the more profound experience of love and grief, joy and suffering, and can afford to be more open and honest with each other.

Michael Mayne

4 | Humanity

To my way of thinking, God trains us, through our disillusionments and mistakes, to understand at last that we must believe only in him and not in men, which places us in the proper position to marvel at all the good which is in men in spite of everything and all the good which they do in spite of themselves.

Jacques Maritain 1882 – 1973

5 | Humility

He that is down need fear no fall,
He that is low no pride.
He that is humble ever shall
Have God to be his guide.

John Bunyan 1628 – 1688

6 | Humility

Humility is an attitude of honesty with God, oneself and all reality. It enables us to be at peace in the presence of our powerlessness and to rest in the forgetfulness of self.

Thomas Keating

7 | Humility

Humility is the acceptance of the truth about ourselves, not an effort to work up humble sentiments in spite of our obvious excellence! It is seeing and accepting the truth that we are not noble, good and spiritual.

Ruth Burrows

8 | Humility

A humble person is one who like the humble Mary says: 'The Lord has done great things for me.' Each of us has an individual greatness. God would not be our author if we were something worthless. You and I and all of us are worth very much, because we are creatures of God, and God has prodigally given his wonderful gifts to every person. And so the Church values human beings and contends for their rights, for their freedom, for their dignity. That is an authentic Church endeavour. While human rights are violated, while there are arbitrary arrests, while there are tortures, the Church considers itself persecuted, it feels troubled, because the Church values human beings and cannot tolerate that an image of God be trampled by persons that become brutalised by trampling on others. The Church wants to make that image beautiful.

Archbishop Oscar Romero 1917– 1980

9 | Humility

O Father, give us the humility which
    Realises its ignorance,
    Admits its mistakes,
    Recognises its need,
    Welcomes advice,
    Accepts rebuke.
Help us always
    To praise rather than to criticise,
    To sympathise rather than to condemn,
    To encourage rather than to discourage,
    To build rather than destroy,
    And to think of people at their best rather than at
      their worst.
    This we ask for thy name's sake.

William Barclay 1907– 1978

10 | Ideals

Blessed is he who carries within himself a God,
an ideal of beauty, and who obeys it;
ideal of art, ideal of science, ideal of the fatherland,
ideal of the virtues of the Gospel,
for therein lie the springs
of great thoughts and great actions;
they all reflect light from the Infinite.

Louis Pasteur 1822 – 1895

11 | If...

If you can keep your head when all about you
    Are losing theirs and blaming it on you,
If you can trust yourself when all men doubt you,
    But make allowance for their doubting too;
If you can wait and not be tired of waiting,
    Or being lied about, don't deal in lies,
Or being hated don't give way to hating,
    And yet don't look too good, or talk too wise;

If you can dream and not make dreams your master;
    If you can think and not make thoughts your aim,
If you can meet with Triumph and Disaster
    And treat those two impostors just the same;
If you can bear to hear the truth you've spoken
    Twisted by knaves to make a trap for fools,
Or watch the things you gave your life to, broken,
    And stoop and build 'em up with worn-out tools;

If you can make one heap of all your winnings;
    And risk it on one turn of pitch and toss,
And lose, and start again at your beginnings
    And never breathe a word about your loss;
If you can force your heart and nerve and sinew
    To serve your turn long after they are gone,

And so hold on where there is nothing in you
    Except the Will which says to them: 'Hold on!'

If you can talk with crowds and keep your virtue,
    Or walk with kings – nor lose the common touch,
If neither foes nor loving friends can hurt you,
    If all men count with you, but none too much;
If you can fill the unforgiving minute
    With sixty seconds' worth of distance run,
Yours is the Earth and everything that's in it,
    And – which is more – you'll be a Man, my son!

Rudyard Kipling 1865 – 1936

12 | Inadequacy

You think because you don't find prayer easy,
    because attendance at Mass is not congenial,
    because your record in the service of God is not
        a good one,
that the things of God are not for you.
Can't you see that the more inadequate you are,
    the more you need God's help?

Cardinal Basil Hume OSB

13 | Individuality

Every individual has a place to fill in the world,
    and is important in some respect,
        whether he chooses to be so or not.

Nathaniel Hawthorne 1804 – 1864

14 | Integrity

Integrity is the completeness of the person within his or her limits. If we become too dependent upon another person or on a set of circumstances, then we lose part of our integrity... At the same time, to become too isolated also means we lose integrity. When we withdraw from other people, when we cut ourselves off from them and say we do not need them, we are deluding ourselves into thinking that there is such a thing as a complete person who doesn't need anybody. If we do not need other people we are not complete.

Dr Tony Lake

15 | Intercessions

I would pray, O Lord, not only for myself but for all the household to which I belong, for all my friends and all my fellow workers, beseeching thee to include them all in thy fatherly regard.

I pray also
> for all who will today be faced by any great
> > decision:
> for all who will today be engaged in settling
> > affairs of moment in the lives of men and
> > nations:
> for all who are moulding public opinion in our
> > time:
> for all who write what other people read:
> for all who are holding aloft the lamp of truth in a
> > world of ignorance and sin:
> for all whose hands are worn with too much toil,
> and for the unemployed whose hands today
> > fall idle.

Let me now go forth, O Lord my God, to the work of another day, still surrounded by thy wonderful loving

kindnesses, still pledged to thy loyal service, still standing in thy strength and not my own.

John Baillie 1886 – 1960

16 Jesus Christ

The borrower

The people of the world have known,
    and still know, their need of a Saviour.
When he comes, he comes as one in need.
He is born in a borrowed stable,
    and learns the trade of a borrowed father.
He eats and sleeps in borrowed homes,
        preaches from borrowed boats,
        enters his capital city on a borrowed donkey.
He shares his last supper in a borrowed room.
Betrayed for borrowed money
        he is aided with his cross by a borrowed shoulder.
Borrows a home for his mother, and is buried
        in a borrowed tomb.
Risen and alive in power, he is still a borrower:
        He wishes to borrow you and me.

17 Jesus Christ

Christ has no body now on earth, but yours,
No hands but yours,
No feet but yours.

Yours are the eyes through which the compassion of
        Christ must look out on the world.
Yours are the feet with which he is to go about
        doing good.
Yours are the hands with which he is to bless
        his people.

St Teresa of Avila 1515 – 1582

18 Jesus Christ

So in Jesus of Nazareth we find a man, subject to all the disabilities and curtailments imposed by his finitude, including the facing and battling with the temptations of his human selfhood. There is all the power he could wield as the political and social revolutionary leader, able to satisfy the needs and desires of his people at the material level, or to restore the glory of the Kingdom of David by freeing his nation, which he loved so deeply, from the Roman yoke; there is the sudden, dramatic act which would focus all eyes upon him, and lend him a supernatural prestige and potency to use in furtherance of the divine ends. Each one has a powerful emotional pull, each calls for a moment of decision at the cost of mind and will and spiritual energy; otherwise the story of the temptation holds no significance. He emerges from those weeks of wrestling, his vision of God clarified and deepened, his whole being open and receptive in his longing to do the will of the Father. All his attention is focused in expectancy to respond to the least impulsion of that will, all his strength is poured out in the love and service of the people around him, in the longing that they may come to share with him, by discovering for themselves, the freedom and joy of the eternal kingdom in which he dwells. So the larger life, the infinite creative power and love and beauty of God could flow into and fill the person and being of the man Jesus, and radiate from him in a way never possible before or since, in a unique act of God in time. In Jesus of Nazareth is found the utmost expression of the infinite and eternal reality of God that is possible within the limits of a human personality, so that Jesus, reaching out to take that life within his own, could declare in and from his manhood: 'He that hath seen me hath seen the Father.'

The vision and existence of God in Christ as something

passionately real, not just a phrase in a creed, strains and tears at the muscles of thought as we strive to apprehend it.

Richenda C. Scott

19 Jesus Christ

Christ is rich, who will maintain you:
He is a King, who will provide you:
He is a sumptuous entertainer, who will feast you.
He is beautiful, who will give you all that can make
    you happy.

St Edmund Campion 1540 – 1581

20 Jesus Christ

It is not said of Jesus that he reached down from on high to pull us up from slavery, but that he became a slave with us. God's compassion is a compassion that reveals itself in servanthood. Jesus became subject to the same powers and influences that dominate us, and suffered our fears, uncertainties and anxieties with us.

Henri Nouwen

21 Jesus Christ

The other gods were strong but
    thou wast weak;
They rode, but thou didst stagger
    to a throne.
But to our wounds only God's
    wounds can speak,
And not a god has wounds but
    thou alone.

E. Shillito

22 | Jesus Christ

When I meditate on the life of Jesus, I see so much of his time spent with uncomprehending people – and his disciples seem to have been remarkably obtuse in understanding his message... But Jesus surely also grew as a person in response to the aggravation he must so often have felt even at the intrusions of his own family during the course of his teaching ministry, so that at the end he could find peace between two criminals crucified on either side of him.

Martin Israel

23 | Jesus Christ

No doubt it is a fine thing to instruct others, but only if the speaker practises what he preaches. One such teacher there is: 'he who spoke the word, and it was done'; and what he achieved even by his silences was well worthy of the Father.

St Ignatius of Antioch   c. 35 – c. 107

24 | Jesus Christ's disciples

Dear Jesus, help me to spread your fragrance everywhere I go. Flood my soul with your spirit and life. Penetrate and possess my whole being so utterly that my life may only be a radiance of yours. Shine through me, and so be in me, that every soul I come in contact with may feel your presence. Let them look up and see no longer me but only Jesus. Stay with me, and then I shall begin to shine as you shine; so to shine as to be a light to others; the light, O Jesus, will be all from you, none of it will be mine; it will be you shining on others through me. Let me praise you in the way you love best by shining on those around me. Let me preach you, not by words only, but by the catching force of example, the evident fullness of the love my heart bears to you.

Mother Teresa of Calcutta

25 Jesus Christ's disciples

The Church wants us to understand that as (God the Son) came once into the world in the flesh, so now, if we remove all barriers, he is ready to come to us again at any minute or hour, to make his home spiritually within us in all his grace.

St Charles Borromeo 1538 – 1584

26 Jesus Christ's presence

In addition to being present in the sacraments, Christ is present in a special manner in every crisis and important event of our lives.

Thomas Keating

27 Jesus Christ's presence

(...) walking along (the road to Emmaus) with a friend I found myself living unforgettably through the experiences of the two travellers who took the same road shortly after the crucifixion, as described in the New Testament. So much so that thenceforth I have never doubted that, wherever the walk and whoever the wayfarers, there is always, as on that other occasion on the road to Emmaus, a third presence ready to emerge from the shadows and fall in step along the dusty, stony way.

Malcolm Muggeridge 1903 – 1990

28 | Jesus Christ's way

Our only task is to keep in step with Jesus. He chooses
the direction and leads the way. As we walk step by
step with him, we soon discover that we have lost the
crushing burden of needing to take care of ourselves
and get our own way, and we discover that the burden
is indeed light.

Richard Foster

29 | Joy

Joy shows from the eyes, it appears when one speaks
and walks. It cannot be kept closed inside us. It reacts
outside. When people find in your eyes that habitual
happiness, they will understand that they are the beloved children of God.

Mother Teresa of Calcutta

30 | Kindness

Keep me, O God, from pettiness.
Let us be large in thought, word and deed.
Let us be done with fault-finding and leave off
    self-seeking.
May we put away all pretence and meet each other
    face to face without self-pity and without
    prejudice.
May we never be hasty in judgment and always
    generous.
Let us make time for all things.
Make us grow calm, serene, gentle.
Teach us to put into action our better impulses, and
    make us straightforward and unafraid.

Grant that we may realise that it is the little things in
life that create differences; that in the big things we
are all one.

And, O Lord God,
Let us not forget to be kind.

Mary Queen of Scots 1542 – 1587

31 Knowledge

Lord Jesus, eternal word of the Father,
you have brought us the good news of the heavenly
Father, and revealed him to us.
Help me, through your word,
to know you and know myself.
Let me see my wretchedness and your mercy,
my sin and your grace,
my poverty and your wealth,
my weakness and your strength,
my folly and your wisdom,
my darkness and your light.

Johann Arndt 1555 – 1621

June

1 | Lent

Lent is a time to learn to travel
light, to clear the clutter
from our crowded lives and
find a space, a
desert.

Deserts are bleak: no creature
Comforts, only a vast expanse of
Stillness, sharpening awareness of
Ourselves and
God.

Ann Lewin

2 | Life

The tree of life

The tree of life is that which has its roots in God.

It is the foundation of all faith
It is the tree of life eternal,
death is but a stem of its beginning and never an end.

It is the crucified Christ
   and the resurrected Messiah.
It is the creation of strength
   and the fortress of power,
for in its branches are the fruits of God
   and the fluorescent spirit of love.
It is the communion of two souls – in heaven and
   on earth.
And the silent presence of God within.

Fleur Dorrell

3 | Life

It is at times when life is threatened – such as times of serious illness – that the Lord gives us a special grace to appreciate 'the gift of life' more deeply as an irreplaceable blessing which only God can give and which God must guide at every step. From the beginning of human life, from conception until death and at every moment in between, it is the Lord our God who gives us life, and we, who are his creatures, should cry out with joy and thanksgiving for this precious gift...

The 'gift of life', God's special gift, is no less beautiful when it is accompanied by illness or weakness, hunger or poverty, mental or physical handicaps, loneliness or old age. Indeed, at this time, human life gains extra splendour as it requires our special care, concern and reverence. It is in and through the weakest of human vessels that the Lord continues to reveal the power of his love.

Cardinal Terence Cooke 1921 – 1983

4 | Life

For there is good news yet to hear
    and fine things to be seen,
Before we go to Paradise
    by way of Kensal Green.

G.K. Chesterton 1874 – 1936

5 | Life

Human life is lived between good and evil. This is where we can see the grandeur of human life. Human beings possess greatness because they can choose, so that in a certain sense even sin testifies that they are great. I am not saying that it testifies to their greatness, just as we cannot say the actions of the Auschwitz executioners testify to their greatness; however, in a certain sense even sin does testify that human beings are great. If this were not so, it would be difficult to understand God's whole relationship with them, with these people who stand between good and evil. God did not cut himself off from mankind because of the tree of the knowledge of good and evil, even though we know that the human race has often exceeded the bounds of this tree. This factor, which is found in the history of mankind and of society, but above all in that of each individual person, has not affected the Creator's great concern for the person who chooses, falls, sins, and rises again. God goes out towards the person, not only as judge, but as Father seeking his prodigal son.

Karol Wojtyla

6 | Life

I have seen the sun break through
to illuminate a small field
for a while, and gone my way
and forgotten it. But that was the pearl
of great price, the one field that had
the treasure in it. I realise now
that I must give all that I have
to possess it. Life is not hurrying
on to a receding future, no hankering after
an imagined past. It is the turning
aside like Moses to the miracle
of the lit bush, to a brightness
that seemed as transitory as your youth
once, but is the eternity that awaits you.

R.S. Thomas

7 | Life

Never cheapen the wonder of the commonplace in life.
God is able to take the common in you and me and
make it a sacrament of blessing for others.

Archbishop George Carey

8 | Life

We come to thee, O God, for thy gracious help. Give us
strength to bear our load of care; give us clearness of
vision so that we may see the wisdom and the love
which have laid it upon us. Help us to be true to our
better selves, to discern our real work in life, and to do
it with all our might. Be by our side when we are
struggling with our own hearts, when we seek to rise
above our failings and weaknesses. Help us to realise
life's meaning, to understand its solemnity, so that each
day we live may be yet another step leading us nearer
to thee. Amen.

Forms of Prayer for Jewish Worship

9 | Life

Lord, in the darkness of my life,
you took me by the hand and
led me into the light.

Lord, in the loneliness of my life,
you took me by the hand and
led me into the fullness of life.

Lord, in the sadness of my life,
you took me by the hand and
showed me the joys of life.

Lord, I am but a poor sinner who
looks to the Light of the world,
for forgiveness and reconciliation.

10 | Listening

You do not have to be clever to please me; all you have
to do is want to love me. Just speak to me as you would
to anyone of whom you are very fond.

Are there any people you want to pray for? Say their
names to me, and ask me as much as you like. I am
generous, but trust me to do what I know is best.

Tell me about your pride, your touchiness, self-
centredness, meanness and laziness. I still love you in
spite of these. Do not be ashamed; there are many
saints in heaven who had the same faults as you; they
prayed to me and, little by little, their faults were
corrected.

Do not hesitate to ask me for blessings for the body and
mind, for health, memory, success. I can give everything.

Tell me about your failures, and I will show you the
cause of them. What are your worries? Who has caused
you pain? Tell me about it. Forgive them, and I will
bless you.

Are you afraid of anything? Have you any tormenting,
unreasonable fears? Trust yourself to me. I am here. I
will not leave you.

Have you no joys to tell me about? Why do you not
share your happiness with me? Tell me what has happened since yesterday to cheer and comfort you. Whatever it was, however big, however small, I prepared it.
Show me your gratitude and thank me.

Are temptations bearing heavily upon you?   Yielding to temptations always disturbs the peace of your soul. Ask me, and I will help you overcome them.

Well, go along now. Get on with your work or play. Try to be humbler, more submissive, kinder; and come back soon and bring me a more devoted heart. Tomorrow I shall have more blessings for you.

Author unknown

11 | Listening

Teach me to listen, Lord,
to those nearest me,
my family, my friends, my co-workers.
Help me to be aware that
no matter what words I hear,
the message is,
'Accept the person I am. Listen to me.'

Teach me to listen, Lord,
to those far from me –
the plea of the forgotten,
the cry of the anguished.

Teach me to listen, Lord,
to myself.
Help me to be less afraid,
to trust the voice inside –
in the deepest part of me.

Teach me to listen, Lord,
for your voice –
in busyness and in boredom,
in certainty and doubt,
in noise and in silence.

Teach me, Lord, to listen.

John Veltri SJ

12 | Listening

... the art of listening is at the heart of genuine prayer. As we learn to listen with attention and sensitivity, all the events of our lives become encounters with the Lord, become prayer.

Thomas H. Green SJ

13 | Listening

It is so easy to spend our times of prayer continuously speaking as we pour out our own needs and desires, but allowing no space for God's words to reach us. It is as necessary in any conversation to listen as to speak, perhaps even more so. The familiar Bible stories reveal that God's word could only be heard by those who were prepared to listen. His is the 'still, small voice', so easy to overlook amid the noise and clamour of our busy lives; all too readily dismissed as something trivial and of no account. God, as the psalmist knew, is everywhere present, in the heights, in the depths and in the uttermost parts of the earth, yet it is possible to live our lives completely oblivious of him. Everything that is of worth must be sought for, and to hear the voice of God will need our very utmost attention and diligence. He will come to us in the silence of our hearts when we have tuned our minds to be receptive to his voice and can shut out all alien sound.

Joan Gibson

14 | Loneliness

If loneliness confines you to the emptiness of a city flat or home, then it is good to remember that Jesus Christ has put his very authentic signature, his mark, his cross, after your name. 'I have chosen you' are his words to all who feel isolated or worthless at the start of each new day.

John J. McCullagh

15 Love

Where you find no love
    put in love
        and you will draw out love.

St John of the Cross 1542 – 1591

16 Love

I confess I can see, but I cannot moderate, nor love as I ought. I pray thee for thy loving kindness' sake supply my want in this particular. And so make me to love all, that I may be a blessing to all: and well pleasing to thee in all. Teach me wisdom, how to expend my blood, estate, life, and time in thy service for the good of all, and make all them that are round about me wise and holy as thou art. That we might all be knit together in Godly love, and united in thy service to thy honour and glory.

Thomas Traherne c. 1636 – 1674

17 Love

If we do a thing because we think it is our duty, we generally fail; that is the old law which makes slaves of us. The real spring of our life, and of our work in life, must be love – true, deep love – not love of this or that person, or for this or that reason, but deep human love, devotion of soul to soul, love of God realised where alone it can be – in love of those whom he loves. Everything else is weak, passes away; that love alone supports us, makes life tolerable, binds the present together with the past and future, and is, we may trust, imperishable.

Max Müller 1823 – 1900

18 Love

We must make no important decision without opening our hearts to love.

19 Love

Learn to love tenderly,
    to love wisely,
        to love courageously:
tenderly so we are not lured away,
    wisely so we do not stumble away,
        courageously, so we are not pushed away
            from the love of the Lord.

St Bernard of Clairvaux 1090 – 1153

20 Love

Written in contemplation

How can we not but love him
Him who first loved us
It is within our hearts to love
To Love what we are a part of

Love is an aching; a longing; a yearning
Love is a looking toward

Love is a power, invisible, yet so strong
Love pulls us. Love draws us

Love enfolds and holds us
Love gives us warmth
Love gives us Peace
Love is an overwhelming joy deep within
Which makes our hearts and souls rejoice

Love is kind and gentle
Love is giving
Love is trust. Love is faith
Love is opening one's heart
Love is submission

Love is a holding
Love is a caring

Love is a brightness – a Radiance – a Glory
Love is devotion

Love gives. Love does not take
Love holds – it does not push away
Love is a brightness – never a gloom

Love is a looking inward to that great Love within
But, yet, a greater looking outward whence to spend
   that Love
That Love, once spent, is soon replenished
Love spent of Love never dies but is continually
   renewed
Love spent of Love is a true Love not a selfish love
Love spent of Love is not for gain but is of Love itself

Love given of Love – a grace
Love given of Love – a gift

Judith Ann Pounder

21 | Love

Love is the fountain and source of friendship.
There can be love without friendship,
but friendship without love is impossible.

St Aelred of Rievaulx 1109 – 1167

22 | Love

It is our duty to love both God and our fellowmen and,
however we may be hindered in other ways, we are
always sufficiently free to wish well to others.

Pope St Leo the Great d. 461

23 | Love

Love is the origin
and source of all good things.

Whoever walks in love
can neither stray nor be afraid.
Love guides, love protects,
love leads to the end.

Christ our Lord has set up
this ladder of love for us
and by it we must climb to heaven.
We must keep a firm hold on love,
we must show it to one another
and by our progress in it,
climb up to heaven.

St Fulgentius 460 – 533

24 | Love

The impulse of love that leads us to the doorway of a friend is the voice of God within and we need not be afraid to follow it.

Agnes Sanford

25 | Love of God

What does it mean to love God? One does not love him the way one loves the persons one sees and touches. For God is not a *person* in our sense of the word. He is the Unknown. He is the wholly Other. He is above terms like *he* and *she; person* and *thing.*

When we say an audience fills the hall and a singer's voice fills the hall, we use the same word to refer to two totally different realities. When we say we love God with our whole heart and love our friend with our whole heart, we also use the same words to express two totally different realities. For the singer's voice does not really fill the hall. And we cannot really *love* God in the usual sense of the word.

To love God with one's whole heart means to say a wholehearted Yes to life and all that life brings with it. To accept, without reservations, all that God has ordained for one's life. To have the attitude that Jesus had when he said: 'Not my will, but yours be done.' To love God with one's whole heart is to make one's own the words made famous by Dag Hammarskjold:

> *For all that has been, Thanks.*
> *To all that shall be, Yes.*

This is the kind of thing one can give only to God. In this he has no rivals. To understand that this is what it means to love God, is to see at once that it doesn't come

91

in the way of your loving friends wholeheartedly, tenderly, passionately.

The singer's voice floods the hall. It remains in undisputed possession of the hall, no matter how packed the hall is with people. The presence of those people is no threat to it. The only threat would come from a rival voice attempting to drown it. God holds undisputed sway over your heart, no matter how many people you have packed into it. The presence of those people is no threat to his love. The only threat would come from an attempt on the part of those people to detract from the wholehearted Yes you say to all God's dispositions for your life.

Anthony de Mello

26 | Love of God

My Lord and my God,
    I believe in you,
    I hope in you,
    I love you with all my heart.

Dom Paul Delatte OSB

27 | Love of God

When a child in his play breaks something valuable, his mother does not love the breakage. But if later on her son goes far away or dies she thinks of the incident with infinite tenderness because she now sees it only as one of the signs of her child's existence. It is in this way that we ought to love God through everything good and everything evil, without distinction. If we love only through what is good, then it is not God we are loving but something earthly to which we give that name. We must not try to reduce evil to good by seeking compensations or justifications for evil. We must love God through the evil that occurs, solely because everything that actually occurs is real and behind all reality stands God. Some realities are more or less transparent; others are completely opaque; but God is behind all of them, without distinction. It is for us simply to keep our eyes turned towards the point where he is, whether we can see him or not. If there were no transparent realities we should have no idea of God. But if all realities were transparent it would not be God but simply the sensation of light that we would be loving. It is when we do not see God, it is when his realities are not sensibly perceptible to any part of our soul, that we have to become really detached from the self in order to love him. That is what it is to love God.

Simone Weil 1909 – 1943

28 Love's demands

Love demands that we know what we can give to others and how we give it and this knowledge can only be derived from our belief in ourselves and in our connection with one another. That belief rests on the fact that when Our Lord told us to love one another he was telling us to do something that could be done. He did not tell us what exactly to do on specific occasions but rather he described a habitual disposition to be maintained by those who would love and be loved.

R.E.C. Browne 1906 – 1975

29 Love's eternity

To love someone, even in the usual human manner, is to get a brief dim glimpse of something within that person which is tremendous, awe-inspiring and eternal. In our ignorance, we think that this 'something' is unique. He or she, we say, is like nobody else. That is because our perception of the Reality is clouded and obscured by the external manifestations – the character and individual qualities of the person we love – and by the way in which our own ego-sense reacts to them. Nevertheless, this weak flash of perception is a valid spiritual experience and it should encourage us to purify our minds and make them fit for that infinitely greater kind of love which always awaits us. This love is not restless or transient, like our human love. It is secure and eternal and calm. It is absolutely free from desire, because lover and loved become one.

Swami Prabharananda and Christopher Isherwood

30 | Love's importance

Be ambitious for the higher gifts. And I am going to show you a way that is better than any of them.

If I have all the eloquence of men or of angels, but speak without love, I am simply a gong booming or a cymbal clashing. If I have the gift of prophecy, understanding all the mysteries there are, and knowing everything, and if I have faith in all its fullness, to move mountains, but without love, then I am nothing at all. If I give away all that I possess, piece by piece, and if I even let them take my body to burn it, but am without love, it will do me no good whatever.

Love is always patient and kind; it is never jealous; love is never boastful, or conceited; it is never rude or selfish; it does not take offence, and is not resentful. Love takes no pleasure in other people's sins but delights in the truth; it is always ready to excuse, to trust, to hope, and to endure whatever comes.

Love does not come to an end... In short there are three things that last: faith, hope and love; and the greatest of these is love.

1 Corinthians 12:31 – 13:1-7.13

July

1 Love's importance

Love takes to itself the life of the loved one.
The greater the love, the greater the suffering of the
    soul.
The fuller the love, the fuller the knowledge of God.
The more ardent the love, the more fervent the
    prayer.
The more perfect the love, the holier the life.

Staretz Silouan

2 Love's meaning

To love a human being means to accept him,
to love him as he is.
Christ's love is like that;
it is entirely disinterested and selfless;
it accepts you as you are,
with all that is displeasing,
disappointing and even painful for him in
you.
If you wait to love a human being
until he has got rid of his faults,
until he is different,
you are only loving an idea.

Julian of Norwich c. 1342 – after 1413

3 Love's meaning

To love someone is to reveal to them their value, and
help them discover that they are precious.

Jean Vanier

4 | Love's meaning

What is love?

No words can define it,
It's something so great,
Only God could design it...
Wonder of wonders,
Beyond man's conception
And only in you
can love find true perfection,
For love is enduring
And patient and kind,
It judges all things,
With the heart not the mind,
And love can transform
The most commonplace
Into beauty and splendour,
And sweetness and grace...
For love is unselfish
Giving more than it takes,
And no matter what happens
Love never forsakes,
It's faithful and trusting
and always believing,
Guileless and honest
and never deceiving...
Yes, love is beyond
What man can define,
For love is IMMORTAL
And God's gift is DIVINE!

5 | Love's strength

For I am certain of this:
neither death nor life.
no angel, no prince, nothing that exists,

nothing still to come, not any power,
or height or depth, nor any created thing,
can ever come between us and the love of God
made visible in Christ Jesus our Lord.

Romans 8:38-39

6 Love's strength

What can separate us from the love of God?

Can sickness or death?
  No nothing can separate us from the love of God.

Can danger or war?
  No nothing can separate us from the love of God.

Can sadness or despair?
  No nothing can separate us from the love of God.

Can the nuclear bomb or the end of the world?
  No nothing can separate us from the love of God.

Can failure or rejection?
  No nothing can separate us from the love of God.

Can loneliness or fear?
  No nothing can separate us from the love of God.

7 Love's strength

And he showed me something small, no bigger than a
hazelnut, lying in the palm of my hand. I looked at it and
thought, what can this be? And I was given this general
answer: it is everything which is made. I was amazed that
it could last because it looked so small and fragile.

And I was answered in my understanding. It lasts and always will, because God loves it and everything has being through the love of God. In this little thing I saw three things: God made it, God loves it, and God cares for it.

Julian of Norwich c. 1342 – after 1413

8 | Marriage

Marriage is not being chained to each other all the time, it's a blessing that one has to guard lovingly and carefully, but not anxiously. It's seeing things through the other's eyes, what does he need now? It's being able to say 'I need you'. It's giving him a present, not because he needs it but because I thought of him when I saw it. God gave us marriage so that we could comfort and help each other; so that we could encourage each other to face the day and its difficulties, the work we do separately or together; so that the person can become what he wants to be, what he is meant to be – and most of all, so that he can be happy. Jonathan went to David, it says in the Old Testament, 'and helped him to find strength in God'. And I know that is what marriage is about in the end – indeed what all human relationships are about.

Hanna Ahrens

9 | Marriage anniversary

God of love,
when we married... years ago
we looked forward with happy expectations
to the joys of love and family life.

There were hurts and disappointments,
but you healed our hurts,

99

and blessed us in ways we hadn't expected.
There were disillusionments and difficulties,
but you gathered us in your loving arms
and shared our burdens.

We thank you, God,
for you have been constantly in our midst.
Your still small voice speaks peace and
encouragement.
Together we have grown
in love, wisdom and understanding.

In quiet faith and confidence
we will walk on with you together.

Rosemary Atkins and others

10 Mary

Magnificat

Tell out, my soul, the greatness of the Lord;
Unnumbered blessings, give my spirit voice;
Tender to me the promise of his word;
In God my Saviour shall my heart rejoice.

Tell out, my soul, the greatness of his name;
Make known his might, the deeds his arm has done;
His mercy sure, from age to age the same;
His holy name, the Lord, the Mighty One.

Tell out, my soul, the greatness of his might;
Powers and dominions lay their glory by.
Proud hearts and stubborn wills are put to flight,
The hungry fed, the humble lifted high.

Tell out, my soul, the glories of his word;
Firm is his promise, and his mercy sure.

Tell out, my soul, the greatness of the Lord
To children's children and for evermore.

Bishop Timothy Dudley-Smith

11 | Mary

'From that hour the disciple took her into his home'

John 19:27

Every time we pause to contemplate and to relive this scene of passion and of love that took place at Calvary we cannot fail to hear the words of Jesus addressed to us entrusting his own mother as our mother. In John, the Church and the believers of all times are present; each one of us is present. 'Behold your Mother'; behold the mother of every man!

When this good mother perceives our limits, she draws near to us to help us even before we ask.

The Lord has given her to us as an advocate, and he gave her the ability to sustain us.

Mary helps the Church that looks to her with trust. With her mercy she sustains those who suffer and risk giving in to discouragement. She looks kindly upon the grave problems that humanity has at this present time.

Pope John Paul II

12 | Mary

Divine love so penetrated and filled the soul of Mary that no part of her was left untouched, so that she loved with her whole heart, with her whole soul, and her whole strength, and was full of grace.

St Bernard of Clairvaux 1090 – 1153

13 | Mary

To look at Mary is to see God's original plan for humanity. In her we see the way God wanted us to be. She is a completely redeemed human being, free from sin and already participating fully in the life of the risen Lord. Mary also shows us how to receive the marvellous gift of God's love, and how to respond to God's redemptive action in our lives. Thus, the closer we come to Mary the better we see the splendour of God's redeemed humanity and the beauty of the redeemed life... There is no other human being in whom we can see so fully what it means to receive the love of a God who loves us so much that he sent his own Son. She has known more blessing and more suffering than anyone else in all humanity. In her we see most fully what it means to be redeemed... Mary's whole being is in the service of Jesus. She is totally Mother, totally given to letting Jesus be born into this world, not only long ago in Bethlehem, but today and always in the heart of anyone who wants to find God. Her whole being is for Jesus. Seeing Mary always means seeing the Mother of God. Knowing Mary always means knowing the one who gives life to God. It is impossible to encounter Mary truly without being led immediately to Jesus. In her, faith finds its purest expression. She is the woman of faith, who always points away from her self to her Son, the source of our redemption.

Henri Nouwen (Andrew Stoecklin)

14 | Mary

The other vision of Mary that I value is her role in the early Church. At prayer with the Twelve, she was there when the Spirit came upon the disciples at Pentecost. Her prayer, her presence must have been a marvellous inspiration to the early Church. I believe that, through the communion of saints, Mary is with every gathering of Christians today. She wants us to come to intimacy with her Son, she continues to say, 'Do as he tells you.' At Cana those who followed that command found water had changed into wine. I believe if we let Mary direct us to Christ then we will experience powerful changes in our life. We will cease to rely on our strength. We will allow grace freedom.

Wilfrid McGreal O Carm

15 Mary

Let us rejoice with the Mother of God,
unite in the chorus of angels
and celebrate this feast of feasts:
the Assumption of the ever-virgin.

On earth she was the treasure and the model of
    virgins;
In heaven she is as one who intercedes for all.
Favourite of God, procuring for us the gifts of the
    Spirit
and with her word teaches wisdom.

The ever virgin Mother of God, our earth blossomed.
While she was on earth, she watched o'er all,
She was like a universal providence
for all the faithful.
Ascended into heaven, interceding for us,
she became a secure refuge for the human race,
near to her Son and God.

Theotekno of Livia

16 Meaning

We misread our fear of meaninglessness. It is not a threat of annihilation, but an invitation to face truth. The facts are kind, and God is in the facts. The fear of our own meaninglessness is saying to us: 'Your defences are ultimately useless. You are wrong in judging your worth by the strength of your useless defences. God alone is your rock, your refuge and your strength. Acknowledge that truth and you will come to know your real worth, for you are precious in his eyes and he loves you. He is calling you to share his own life.'

Gerard W. Hughes SJ

17 Meeting God

Meeting God can be very simple. If it is not simple, and no voice speaks in our silence, and no hand reaches down to meet ours in trust, then we should ask ourselves these questions, for the mistake may be ours.

Perhaps God cannot be himself to us, because we are not ourselves, our true selves, to him. We have not prayed to him as we are, but as we feel we ought to be, or as others want us to be, or as what we think he thinks we ought to be. This last is the most difficult to unravel because it hides a confusion or a blasphemy.

Perhaps God meets us and we do not recognise him. He may speak to us in a chance remark we overhear, through a stray thought in our mind, or by a word from the prayerbook that resonates in us. Perhaps a side door is the only door we have left open to him. The others we defended and barred, so he must steal into us as a thief in the night.

Perhaps we do not like what he says, but are frightened to say so, and so pretend we never met him, and indeed could not meet him, for he is only an idea. The avoidance is natural because in the sight of God our success can seem failure, and our ambitions dust.

Perhaps we are satisfied with our lives and do not want to meet him. So we chant our prayers and sing our hymns to prevent a few moments' silence, for he speaks in the silence.

Perhaps we have not allowed God to judge us because we have already judged him, and anticipated his word. He may love us more than we know: he may know us better than we know ourselves; he may still surprise us.

Perhaps we are frightened where he may lead us. He may send us from our father's house; he may bring us to the wilderness; he may let us wander in it for forty years; he may ask us to find our security in what we cannot touch. Will he give us courage equal to our need if we pray?

Meeting God can be simple, but nothing can happen if we do not will it. If we seek the Lord he can be found; he will allow us to find him if we seek him with all our might.

Rabbi Lionel Blue

18 | Meeting God

How can we turn our knowledge about God into knowledge of God? The rule for doing this is demanding, but simple. It is that we turn each truth that we learn *about* God into matter for meditation *before* God, leading to prayer and praise *to* God.

J.I. Packer

19 Mental prayer

Mental prayer in my opinion is nothing else than an intimate sharing between friends; it means taking time frequently to be alone with him who we know loves us best.

St Teresa of Avila 1515 – 1582

20 Mercy

Almighty Lord God,
your glory cannot be approached,
your compassion knows no bounds,
and your love for all mankind
is beyond all human expression;
in your mercy
look upon us
and all your people
but deal with us according to your goodness.
Guide us to the haven of your will
and make us truly obedient
to your commandments,
that we may not feel ashamed
when we come before your Messiah's dread judgment
     seat.

For you, O God,
are good and ever-loving,
and we glorify you,
Father, Son, and Holy Spirit,
now and for ever,
to the ages of ages. Amen.

Prayer of the Orthodox Tradition

21 | Mercy

I have become convinced that the very contradictions in my life are in some ways signs of God's mercy to me; if only because someone so complicated and so prone to confusion and self-defeat could hardly survive for long without special mercy.

Thomas Merton 1915 – 1968

22 | Mercy

Mercy is one of the greatest acts the human heart is capable of. Its source is love. If love has become really deep rooted in a person, that is, if it has taken possession of his body and soul and of his whole being, then at the same time it has made him liable to suffer. People are astonishingly quick to notice the unselfish and generous heart. From selfless love, they seek help and above all the warmth of human affection: the hungry seek food, the thirsty ask for a drink, the naked for clothing, the stranger for a home, the captive for release; the sick ask to be cared for and the dying ask for comfort, the unrighteous desire patience, the ignorant ask to be taught, the sorrowful seek consolation, and all men, the living and the dead, call for prayer. It is customary to speak of the seven works of mercy. They are a visible expression of all the misery of human existence.

To take this misery upon ourselves brings suffering with it, sometimes unbearable suffering. The distress of others takes more out of us than does our own suffering. Our existence is threatened more by the frailty of others than by our own weakness. The helplessness of someone who is suffering is often too much for us. Someone comes to us with his face drawn with his suffering, and we are powerless and unable to help. There still remains one final work of mercy, that cannot simply be equated with the other seven because it is the basis of all mercy. When suffering goes really deep, one can often only help by 'sympathising', sharing in the suffering. The only thing one is still able to do is to open one's heart, let the suffering of the other person pour in, and persevere in sharing in his suffering, until he finds that his suffering is relieved because someone who loves him is sharing the burden. Anyone who thinks it is easy to persevere in love to the bitter end in this way, so that this becomes the most characteristic act of life, does not yet know the profundity of human love.

Ladislaus Boros

23 Mercy

How often has it happened that what we consider a punishment and chastisement of God, was a special work of grace, an act of his infinite mercy!

St Alphonsus Liguori 1698 – 1787

24 Missionaries

A missionary's Nunc Dimittis

Lord, it is time for me to go home.
I want it to be a quiet, peaceful going as you promised.
No fuss, no bother, just to slip away quietly.
And I go away, Lord, far beyond my wildest dreams,
my eyes have seen the salvation you have prepared
in the sight of many peoples:
the Turkanas, the Pocots, the Buganda, and the rest.
I have seen your light shine in the darkness,

I have shared the light of your light-bringers,
your missionaries;
I have shared their joys, their sorrows, and their love.
I have seen your glory as you joined the nations
to your chosen Israel, the people you have made
your own.
And so it is time for me to go, Lord.
Time to go home to you, and as I go
my prayer is that I shall meet them all again
in the Kingdom where your missionaries will receive
the hundred-fold you promised to those
who would leave everything – even their very selves –
that they might be your witnesses in Jerusalem,
in all Judaea, and Samaria, and even
to the farthest of earth's bounds.
Lord, it is time for me to go,
and may my going be in peace.

James Good

25 | Morning prayer

O Lord, my Father, my Creator, my Friend,
Thank you for this new day.
Thank you for those who love me, and care for me.
Thank you for the wonder of my being,
For gifts of mind, heart and body.
Thank you for all the good things I enjoy
And the trials which make me strong.

Help me, O Lord,
To make the best of every hour of this day.
Save me from fear, selfishness and greed.
Help me to enjoy
    the love I receive,
And to share my love with a glad and generous heart.

May no one suffer today because of me;
May no one go hungry because of my greed;
May no one be lonely because I do not care.
May my heart be open to those who need me.

May I grow in strength, in joy, in love today,
May I seek what is true, noble and pure.
May I begin and end this day in your presence,
And walk through my life secure, for I'm never alone.
Thank you, Lord, for your love, presence and
    protection.
Thank you for guarding me as the apple of your eye.

Sister Joan

26 Nature

Look to the mountains –
    to the greatness God has made –
        therein lies comfort,
            therein lies inner strength,
                therein lies peace of mind.

Anon.

27 Need

God stands in no need of anyone else,
but man stands completely in need of God.

St Irenaeus c. 130 – c. 200

28 Night prayer

At the end of another day of grace,
May my heart open in praise and thanks to you, my
    God;

Thank you, Lord,
For this day of life,
For all that it brought me –
The opportunities I have been given,
The people I have met,
The conversations I have had,
The knowledge I have gained,
The love I have received and given.

I look back upon the joys experienced,
at the tasks I was able to complete,
at the satisfaction I experienced.

I also look at my disappointment and failures,
at the jobs unfinished,
at the pain I caused,
at the good I left undone,
at the memories that still hurt.

Lord, open my eyes to the wonders you
    worked today in the world and in me.
Open my heart to accept
    your pardon and your peace.
Teach me to end this day
    in trustful surrender.

In you I trust;
To you I belong.
To you I entrust
    all those who died today
    and their dear ones who mourn;
    those who are on their death bed right now.

I remember those who work all night,
    all travellers, and those in charge of their safety;
    all those who have had a difficult day,
    or fear the oncoming night;
    all those who are in pain
    or too lonely to rest or to pray.

May these evening hours
    prepare me for the great evening of my life,
When I will look back on life's day
    and find no words
    to thank you
    for all the love I will have received.

Sister Joan

29 | Night prayer

A prayer written for Evensong intercessions

O Lord!
    Be with those who watch this night
O Lord!
    Be with those who wait

Those who watch with the suffering
    Be thou their eyes
Those who wait with the dying
    Be thou their arms
Those who watch in silence
    Be thou their succour
Those who wait in fear
    Be thou their strength
Those who watch and wait with loved ones
    Be thou their compassion
Those who watch and wait alone
    Be thou their friend

O Lord!
    We pray, be the comfort of all who watch and wait
        this night
O Lord!
    We pray, be thou their Peace. Amen

Judith Ann Pounder

30 | Obedience

Every increase in our knowledge of God is a demand for further obedience to him. He does not compel obedience to him; the urgency of the demand is generated by love, and love is not marked by our passivity but by active response to him in whom all love begins, in whom all power has its source.

R.E.C. Browne 1906 – 1975

31 | Old age

When you are old and grey and full of sleep,
And nodding by the fire, take down this book,
And slowly read, and dream of the soft look
Your eyes had once, and of their shadows deep;

How many loved your moments of glad grace,
And loved your beauty with love false or true,
But one man loved the pilgrim soul in you,
And loved the sorrows of your changing face;

And bending down beside the glowing bars,
Murmur, a little sadly, how Love fled
And paced upon the mountains overhead
And hid his face amid a crowd of stars.

W.B. Yeats 1865 – 1939

August

1 | Old age

Perhaps you have at one time or another, walked over a field which has just been harvested. The crop has been lifted, the corn has been reaped, all that remain are the stalks cut within a few inches of the soil, the clods of earth and the inevitable weeds sprouting up. Well, that is how we should look at some people's lives. Our life isn't always just where we think it is. Gradually, as the days go by, our life is gathered by God. When we see a life, when we have the impression that it is failing, we must say, as of the harvested field: the crop isn't there any more, it's not lost, it's in the barn, it's somewhere else... This life which seems lost amidst the afflictions of old age, has not been wasted, it is the harvested field. This life is elsewhere, in the memory and the heart of God.

Phillippe Zeissig

2 | Others

We cannot know whether we love God, although there may be strong reasons for thinking so, but there can be no doubt about whether we love our neighbour or not.

St Teresa of Avila 1515 – 1582

3 | Others

One other thing stirs me when I look back at my youthful days, viz. the fact that so many people were something to me without knowing it. Such people, with whom I never perhaps exchanged a word, yet, and others about whom I merely heard things by report, had a decisive influence on me; they entered into my life and became powers within me. Much that I should otherwise not have felt so clearly or done so effectively was felt or done as it was, because I stand, as it were, under the sway of these people. Hence I always think that we all live, spiritually, by what others have given us in the significant hours of our life. These significant hours do not announce themselves as coming, but arrive unexpected. Nor do they make a great show of themselves; they pass almost unperceived. Often indeed, their significance comes home to us first as we look back, just as the beauty of a piece of music or of a landscape often strikes us first in our recollection of it. Much that has become our own in gentleness, modesty, kindness, willingness to forgive, in veracity, loyalty, resignation under suffering, we owe to people in whom we have seen or experienced those virtues at work, sometimes in a great matter, sometimes in a small. A thought which had become act sprang into us like a spark, and lighted a new flame within us...

If we had before us those who have thus been a blessing to us, and could tell them how it came about, they would be amazed to learn what passed over from their life to ours.

Albert Schweitzer 1875 – 1965

4 | Pain

God whispers to us in our pleasures,
    speaks in our conscience,
        but shouts in our pains.
It is his megaphone to rouse a deaf world.

C.S. Lewis 1898 – 1963

5 │ Parenting

For my daughter

Even though we don't always see things eye to eye,
I hope you always remember how much
I care about you,
as your words and actions have proven
how you care about me too.
And even though it sometimes seems
as if we're out of touch
and don't always understand each other,
the bond between us runs much deeper –
the love between us finds a way to understand
what the eyes and ears cannot.

Anon.

6 │ Patience

Be patient with everyone, but above all with yourself. I mean, do not be disheartened by your imperfections, but always rise up with fresh courage. I am glad you make a fresh beginning daily; there is no better means of attaining to the spiritual life than by continually beginning again, and never thinking that we have done enough. How are we to be patient in bearing with our neighbour's faults, if we are impatient in bearing with our own? He who is fretted by his own failings will not correct them; all profitable correction comes from a calm, peaceful mind.

St Francis de Sales 1567– 1622

7 | Patience

Wait with patience
    for the moments
    of the good God –

Everything needs time.

The good God can give more
    than our idea can conceive.

The whole thing
    is to have
    great confidence in
    the good God.

St Julie Billiart 1751 – 1816

8 | Patience

... give God a chance. Take your problem, whatever it may be, to him in prayer. Tell him all about it – just as if he didn't know a thing. In the telling be absolutely honest and sincere. Hold nothing back... believe that God will hear you... Next, you must be willing to wait patiently for the Lord. He does not answer every prayer on Sunday afternoon. You may have to wait until Friday. But wait. God is never in a hurry... (The reply) generally comes through our own conscience in a sort of growing conviction that such and such a course of action is the one he wants you to take. Or it may be given you in the advice of friends of sound judgment... God speaks sometimes through our circumstances and guides us, closing doors as well as opening them.

Peter Marshall 1902 – 1949

9 | Peace

Peace I leave with you; my peace I give to you;
not as the world gives do I give to you.
Let not your hearts be troubled,
neither let them be afraid.

John 14:27

10 | People of God

The eyes of faith behold a wonderful scene: that of a
countless number of lay people, both men and women,
busy at work in their daily life and activity, oftentimes
far from view and quite unacclaimed by the world,
unknown to the world's great personages but nonethe-
less looked upon in love by the Father, untiring labour-
ers who work in the Lord's vineyard. Confident and
steadfast through the power of God's grace, these are
the humble yet great builders of the Kingdom of God in
history.

Pope John Paul II

11 | Perfection

Perfection consists not in spiritual consolations but in an
increase of love. On this too will depend our reward –
as well as on the goodness and the truth shown forth in
our actions.

St Teresa of Avila 1515 – 1582

12 | Perspective

Looking back on my journey so far, dear Lord, I see
how your love and goodness have been with me,

through many failings and dangers, in many joys and adventures. I have received much love from friends, been guided and inspired by the wisdom and encouragement of many teachers and writers. Often I have felt your presence near, and sometimes I have had to walk by faith. Forgive my slowness, my failures in faith, the smallness of my love, my poor use of your grace. Accept my heart's thanks for growing knowledge of you, for increasing assurance of your loving purpose and deepening understanding of the things that are eternal. As I turn again to the journey ahead, it is bright with the remembrances of past mercies, O dear and gracious Father and Saviour.

George Appleton

13 | Perspective

When we lose our sense of awe and wonder at the wholly otherness of God, we soon begin to distort the scale. We grow greater, and God grows smaller.

Delia Smith

14 | Perspective

I recognise, of course, that any statement of belief from me is partly governed by the fact that I am old, and in a decade or so will be dead. In earlier years I should doubtless have expressed things differently. Now the prospect of death overshadows all. I am like a man on a sea voyage nearing his destination. When I embarked I worried about having a cabin with a porthole, whether I should be asked to sit at the captain's table, who were the more attractive and important passengers. All such considerations become pointless now that I shall soon disembark.

Since I do not believe that earthly life can bring lasting satisfaction, the prospect of death holds no terrors. But the world that I shall leave seems more beautiful than ever, especially its remoter parts: grass and trees, little streams and sloping hills, where the image of eternity is more clearly stamped than among streets and houses. Those I love I can love even more, since I have nothing to ask of them but their love; the passion to accumulate possessions, or to be noticed and important, is now too evidently absurd to be entertained.

A sense of how extraordinarily happy I have been, and of enormous gratitude to my creator, overwhelms me. I believe with a passionate unshakable conviction that life is a blessed gift; that the spirit which animates it is one of love not hate, of light not darkness.

Since I believe also that life is benevolently, not malevolently, conceived, then I know that when these eyes see no more and this mind thinks no more, and this hand now writing is inert, I shall find what lives beyond similarly benevolent. If that is nothing, then for nothingness I offer thanks; if it is another mode of existence, then for that likewise, I offer thanks.

Malcolm Muggeridge 1903 – 1990

15 | Pity

Sunday visit

We finally found him
curled up in the chair like a many-wrinkled shell
staring blindly out at nothing
among a gathering of imbecilic fossils
his one good eye fastening fiercely onto life
the hair still sturdy though silver under the old
    cloth cap.

We finally found him
through all that terrible labyrinth of grey concrete cells
quietly rounding out his days
alone in a morass of moronic camaraderie
his doomed cell mates snoozing and snoring
     all around
and he with his one good eye defying the shadows.

The tears came then
not soft, but real
the tears of a real man broken by life
groping wildly with gnarled fingers at the straws of life
in that awful room of no life
and the television set blaring forth its banalities
drowning whatever words of comfort our futile
     tongues could offer.

I had no words for him
no words to span the heartbreak years
when Samson-like he had stood between us and chaos
bringing to us the small rare trinkets of his love.
I had for him only whiskey
the old bitter gift
the poor tribute of one poorer in spirit
than that jaded near-blind half-dead soul reclining so
     tamely
in a wicker chair
in a ward of fearful paralysing resignation
a ward full of already dead people
sleeping as the television blared.

Yet the hand that gripped mine spelled out love
and the raw lovely courage of that old landscaped face
put my feeble pity to shame.

Christy Brown

16 Poverty

We have already noted that, to the infinite scandal of all respectable people, Jesus chose his friends among the poor, the alienated, the underprivileged and the socially discarded. It was taken for granted that a religious teacher would move in the society of the virtuous, the polished and the well-to-do and that he would become interested in the others only when they had reached a certain stage in the transformation of themselves into respectability. Jesus swept away all such prudential ideas with the one trenchant maxim, 'They that are whole have no need of a physician, but they that are sick.' He seems really to have liked his disreputable friends and to have found among them a sincerity and an openness to the realities of life that are often lacking among those whose existence has been cushioned against those harsh realities. He was prepared to accept them in their pathetic absurdity, their alienation from society, and the darkening of their minds and spirits. They could not wear out his patience; stupid, inconstant and faithless; they found him changeless and always the same. He was prepared to trust them even when they were not worthy of any trust.

Stephen Neill

17 Poverty

Who are the poor?

The poor are the materially and spiritually destitute.
The poor are the hungry and thirsty.
The poor are those who need clothing.
The poor are the homeless and the harbourless.
The poor are the sick.
The poor are the physically and mentally handicapped.
The poor are the aged.

The poor are those imprisoned.
The poor are the lonely.
The poor are the ignorant and the doubtful.
The poor are the sorrowful.
The poor are the comfortless.
The poor are the helpless.
The poor are the persecuted.
The poor are those who suffer injustice.
The poor are the ill-mannered.
The poor are the bad-tempered.
The poor are the sinners and scoffers.
The poor are those who do us wrong.
The poor are the unwanted, the outcasts of society.
The poor are somehow or other –
    we ourselves.

Co-workers of Mother Teresa

18 | Poverty

The poor are all the people who have to put up with violence and injustice without being able to defend themselves. The poor are all the people who have to exist on the very fringe of death, with nothing to live from and nothing to live for. But in Jesus' message the poor are surely all of us too, since we have nothing to offer the coming God except the burden of our guilt and the rags of our exile – like the Prodigal Son.

Jurgen Moltmann

19 | Poverty

We must remember that all we possess is a gift. The first beatitude is one of poverty, and only if we live according to this beatitude can we enter into the kingdom of God. This beatitude has two aspects. First, there is the very clear fact that we possess nothing which we can keep, whether we want to or not; it is the discovery that I am nothing and that I have nothing – total, irremediable, hopeless poverty. We exist because we have been willed into existence and brought into existence. We have done nothing for it, it was not an act of our free will. We do not possess life in such a way that it is impossible for anyone to take it away from us, and all that we are and all that we possess is ephemeral in this way. We have a body – it will die. We have a mind – yet it is enough for one minute vessel to burst in a brain for the greatest mind to be suddenly extinguished. We have a heart, sensitive and alive – and yet a moment comes when we would like to pour out all our sympathy, all our understanding for someone who is in need, and at that moment there is nothing but a stone in our breast.

So, in a way, we can say that we possess nothing because we are masters of nothing which is in our possession. And this could lead us, not to the sense of belonging to the kingdom of God and rejoicing in it, but to despair – if we did not remember that although none of these things are ours in such a way that they cannot be taken away from us, yet we are in possession of them. This is the second aspect of the beatitude. We are rich, and everything which we possess is a gift and a sign of the love of God and the love of men, it is a continuous gift of divine love; and as long as we possess nothing, love divine is manifested continuously and fully. But everything we take into our own hands to possess is taken out of the realm of love. Certainly it becomes ours, but love is lost. And it is only those who give everything away who become aware of true, total, final, irremediable, spiritual poverty, and who possess the love of God expressed in all his gifts...

This is the Kingdom, the sense that we are free from possession, and this freedom establishes us in a rela-

tionship where everything is love – human love and
divine love.

Metropolitan Anthony of Sourozh

20 Poverty

If I love, if I really love, how can I tolerate the fact that a
third of humanity is menaced with starvation while I
enjoy the security of economic stability? If I act in that
way I shall perhaps be a good Christian, but I shall
certainly not be a saint; and today there are far too
many good Christians when the world needs saints. We
must learn to accept instability, put ourselves every now
and then in the condition of having to say, 'Give us this
day our daily bread,' with real anxiety because the
larder is empty; have the courage, for love of God and
one's neighbour, to give until it hurts and, above all,
keep open in the wall of the soul the great window of
living faith in the Providence of an all-powerful God.

Carlo Carretto

21 Praise

The praise of God should be the object of our meditation in this life, because in the life to come it will be for
ever the object of our rejoicing.

St Augustine 354 – 430

22 Praise

Father, all-powerful and ever-living God,
we do well always and everywhere to give you thanks.

You have no need of our praise,
yet our desire to thank you is itself your gift.

Our prayer of thanksgiving adds nothing to your
    greatness,
but makes us grow in your grace,
through Jesus Christ our Lord.

Preface of Weekdays IV – Roman Missal

23 | Prayer

Prayer activity can be no substitute for time set aside
exclusively for God. How sad it is that prayer in this
sense is not part and parcel of the normal Christian life,
and yet without it one cannot be fully Christian.

Ruth Burrows

24 | Prayer

God does not ask us to tell him our needs
that he may learn about them,
but that we may be capable of receiving
what he is preparing to give.

St Augustine 354 – 430

25 | Prayer

O Lord, thinking about you, being fascinated with theo-
logical ideas and discussion, being excited about histories
of spirituality and stimulated by thoughts and ideas about
prayer and meditation, all of this can be as merely
expressive of greed as the unruly desire for food, possessions, or power. Each day I see again that only you can
let me dwell in your presence. No book, no idea, no
concept or thing, will ever bring me close to you, unless
you yourself let these instruments become the way to you.

Henri Nouwen

26 | Prayer

I know, my God, that my prayer need not be enthusiastic and ecstatic to succeed in placing me so much in your power and at your disposal that nothing is held back from you. Prayer can be real prayer, even when it is not filled with blessings and jubilation or the shining brilliance of a carefree surrender of self.

Karl Rahner SJ 1904 – 1984

27 | Prayer

I have lived my life, and that which I have done
May he within himself make pure! but thou,
If thou should'st never see my face again,
Pray for my soul. More things are wrought by prayer
Than this world dreams of. Wherefore let thy voice
Rise like a fountain for me night and day.
For what are men better than sheep or goats
That nourish a blind life within the brain,
If, knowing God, they lift not hands of prayer
Both for themselves and those who call them friend?

From Morte D'Arthur
Alfred Lord Tennyson 1809 – 1892

28 | Prayer

Lord, teach me to pray, to want to pray, to delight to pray. When I pray, teach me to pray with faith, with hope, with love. Let me make prayer my first work, my persistent work, my most important work; work that I do for you, for others, for the whole world. Let my prayer be a channel for your love, your grace, your peace for those for whom I pray, and for myself, O dear and blessed Lord.

Eric Milner-White d. 1963

29 | Prayer

The desire to pray is itself a clear sign of the Lord's presence. We cannot reach out to him unless he first draws us. Since he is Lord, since he cares more for us than we do for ourselves, he would never plant this desire in us merely to frustrate us. He would never lead us to seek something which was impossible.

Thomas H. Green SJ

30 | Prayer

Let us keep in mind that in prayer we are, with Jesus, the world's ambassadors to the Father. All mankind needs to find its voice in our prayer: it is a matter of mankind needing redemption, forgiveness, purification. Moreover, in our prayer we must also include what troubles us, what shames us, what by its nature separates us from God, but which belongs to our weakness or to the poverty of our individual persons. This is how Peter prayed after the miraculous catch of fish, saying to Jesus: 'Leave me, Lord. I am a sinful man.' (Luke 5:8).

This prayer, which is born from the humility of the experience of sin, and which feels united with the moral poverty of all mankind, touches God's merciful heart and renews in the conscience of the one praying the attitude of the prodigal son, who moved his father's heart.

Pope John Paul II

31 | Prayer – a necessity

Prayer shows us that life makes little sense if this is all it is: making money, making love, making a name for ourselves, making idols. The poverty of affluence, the failure of success, the emptiness of material plenty, the moral laziness of being busy – all these only make us hungry for something deeper. They drive us to a new concern for our inner needs, for friendships that last, and for spiritual resources that strengthen us inside. They make us long for a personal relationship with God to replace the emptiness of modern life.

James Houston

September

1 | Prayer and contemplation

There is a widespread impression that the gift of contemplation is an abnormal phenomenon in human life,
restricted to a few especially chosen souls, most of
whom withdraw completely from everyday life. But
while this gift of contemplation in its fullness is the
crown of spiritual life and the direct gift of God alone,
it should in some sense be the goal of all who seek
God, and it is granted to a greater or lesser degree to all
who earnestly seek to love God with all their heart,
mind, soul and strength, this degree depending upon
the soul's progress in the life of prayer. Prayer is mankind's highest activity, and like all other activities
develops from small beginnings and reaches its goal in
many varied ways. The intensity of the love of one
human being for another is dependent upon the degree
to which the loved one occupies the heart and mind
of the lover; similarly, the intensity of man's love and
the depth of his experience of God depends upon the
degree to which God occupies the heart and mind of
one who seeks him. When a man devotes himself to
know and love God with his whole heart, mind, soul
and strength, God grants his gift of love and contemplation, through and in which lover and Beloved are
united.

Leo Sherley Price

2 | Prayer as gift

Prayer is ultimately a gift to us, a gift of God, so it is
better to go to prayer with empty hands. For if our
hands are full of good works which we joyfully offer up
to God, there is no room for God to put anything in
them. At times we have to be able to set everything
aside and forget it: all our duties and tasks, all our own

130

plans, in order to be able to go to God completely naked, simply to receive. Then the Lord will surprise us, astound us, shake us, for he will fill our hands to overflowing. We shall receive treasure beyond our dreams. But in prayer one first has to have the experience of radical poverty.

Henri Boulad SJ

3 | Prayer of attention

The immediate person thinks and imagines that when he prays, the important thing, the thing he must concentrate upon, is that God should hear what he is praying for. And yet, in the true, eternal sense it is just the reverse: the true relation in prayer is not when God hears what is prayed for, but when the person praying continues to pray until he is the one who hears what God wills. The immediate person, therefore, makes demands in his prayer: the true man of prayer only attends.

Sören Kierkegaard 1813 – 1855

4 | Prayer of Jesus

The central message of the New Testament is that there is really only one prayer and that this prayer is the prayer of Christ. It is a prayer that continues in our hearts day and night... (It is) the stream of love that flows constantly between Jesus and his Father. (It) is the Holy Spirit.

It is the most important task for any fully human life that we should become as open as possible to this stream of love. We have to allow this prayer to become our prayer, we have to enter into the experience of being swept beyond ourselves into this wonderful prayer of Jesus – this great cosmic river of love.

In order for us to do this we must learn... a most demanding (discipline that is a way of silence and stillness.) It is as though we have to create a space within ourselves that will allow... the consciousness of the prayer of Jesus to envelop us in this powerful mystery.

Many Christians have lost touch with their own tradition of prayer. We no longer benefit as we should from the wisdom and experienced counsel of the great masters of prayer. These masters have agreed that in prayer it is not we ourselves who take the initiative. We are not talking to God. We are listening to his word within us. We are not looking for him; it is he who has found us.

Dom John Main OSB 1926 – 1986

5 | Prayer, the practice

The only way to pray – is to pray; and the way to pray well is to pray much. If one has not time for this, then one must at least pray regularly. But the less one prays, the worse it goes. And if circumstances do not permit even regularity, then one must put up with the fact that when one does try to pray, one can't pray – and our prayer will probably consist of telling this to God.

Dom John Chapman OSB 1865 – 1933

6 | Prayer, the practice

When you pray, you yourself must be silent.
You do not pray to have your own earthbound desires fulfilled, but you pray: thy will be done.

It is not fitting to wish to use God as an errand boy. You yourself must be silent; let the prayer speak.

Tito Colliander

7 Prayer, the practice

The greatest miracle of all is prayer. I have only to turn my thoughts to God and I suddenly feel a strength which bursts into me from somewhere, bursts into my soul, into my entire being. What is it? Psychotherapy? No, it is not psychotherapy, for where would I, an insigniicant old man who is tired of life, get this strength which renews me and saves me, lifting me above the earth? It comes from without, and there is no force on earth that can even understand it.

Anatoli Levitin

8 Prayer unceasing

The principal thing is to stand before God with the intellect in the heart, and to go on standing before him unceasingly day and night, until the end of life.

Bishop Theophan

9 Prayer unceasing

There is one thing in prayer that we all need so greatly... a few minutes each day of peace and quiet with oneself, at least a minute fragment of the day to listen within oneself, attending to the voice of God.

Ellen Littmann

10 | Prayer's effects

If we are generous in giving time to prayer, we will experience its benefits throughout our life.

St John Chrysostom c. 347– 407

11 | Prayer's language

The language of prayer is learned like any other language: by effort, application and practice. But underneath all these is the question, 'Do you want this inner conversation?' If we want it enough, we will get it. The answer is in the will...

It is not difficult to produce a mystical moment. The difficulty lies in recognising it and keeping it, and persevering through non-mystical hours, days or years.

Rabbi Lionel Blue

12 | Prayer's meaning

Believe and trust that as it is easy for you to breathe the air and live by it, or to eat and drink, so it is easy and even still easier for your faith to receive all spiritual gifts from the Lord. Prayer is the breathing of the soul; prayer is our spiritual food and drink.

John of Cronstadt 1829– 1908

13 | Prayer's meaning

Prayer is not asking.
    It is a longing of the soul.
        It is a daily admission of one's weakness...

It is better in prayer to have a heart without words
than words without a heart.

Mahatma Gandhi 1869 – 1948

14 | Present moment

Let us then think only of the present, and not even
permit our minds to wander with curiosity into the
future. This future is not yet ours; perhaps it never will
be. It is exposing ourselves to temptation to wish to
anticipate God, and to prepare ourselves for things
which he may not destine for us. If such things should
come to pass, he will give us light and strength according to the need. Why should we desire to meet difficulties prematurely, when we have neither strength nor
light as yet provided for them: Let us give heed to the
present, whose duties are pressing; it is fidelity to the
present which prepares us for fidelity in the future.

François Fénelon 1651 – 1715

15 | Present moment

The present moment is like an ambassador who de-
clares the Will of God to me.

Jean-Pierre de Caussade 1675 – 1751

16 | Present moment

The great spiritual teachers of all religions have themselves practised and taught mindfulness.

To be mindful is to live in the present moment, not to
be imprisoned in the past nor anticipating a future that
may never happen.

When we are fully aware of the present, life is transformed and strain and stress disappear.

So much of modern life is a feverish anticipation of future activity and excitement. We have to learn to step back from this into the freedom and possibility of the present.

Dom Bede Griffiths OSB

17 | Present moment

(Today) is a gift from God which holds out immense opportunities for us. It is the first day of the rest of our lives; whatever yesterday was like, today is wholly new and the future lies ahead.

Bishop David Hope

18 | Priesthood

Ours is a wonderful vocation and we must be proud to be priests. It must be evident to others that we are proud of our priesthood and that we treasure especially our responsibility in the Word of God, in the sacraments, and quite especially in the Eucharist. People instinctively recognize what it means to us. They know if we love the Word of God, if we love the sacraments, if we love the Mass.

Celebrating the Mass for and with our people, speaking to them a word of love and encouragement, meeting them in their homes and your parishes as you do – surely there is no greater calling in life, so full of possibilities and so rewarding?

Cardinal Basil Hume OSB

19 | Priesthood

A priest who is a man of faith and prayer is able to be truly a man of service because he has a vision of God and of his kingdom. Prayer is among other things the motivation, the contemplation of that vision. Our priestly prayer is both the exercise of our faith and the nourishment of our faith. Therefore, every priest must make the daily effort to persevere in faith and love, in private prayer, liturgical worship and pastoral service. It will continue to be a daily struggle to achieve a balanced integrity in private prayer, liturgical worship and pastoral service. But without that balance our priestly lives will suffer and we will not enjoy the abundant spiritual life that is our heritage.

... The priesthood of Jesus is a call to worship – and especially to the one supreme act of worship, the Eucharist. There were many things that Jesus would ask of his apostles: to preach the gospel, to forgive sinners, to feed the hungry and clothe the naked, to take up their cross and follow him – but he made them priests by changing bread and wine into his body and blood so that people would share in his sacrifice till the end of time – and then saying to these twelve men: 'Do *this* in memory of me.' It means that no matter how much a priest works to care for the poor and console the suffering and to build a better world, the supreme moment of his priesthood – the one that gives him the strength and the inspiration and the sense of the closeness of Christ to carry on in all the others – comes when he takes bread and wine into his hands and makes the redeeming sacrifice of Jesus present in a Christian community so that the community may make that sacrifice its own.

Cardinal Terence Cooke 1921 – 1983

20 | Priesthood

One of the great joys of the priesthood is to give communion to your people – his people – the ones you know as their pastor. Becoming part of their lives, you know that this man is divorced and heart-broken; this woman is spending her life in the service of her handicapped child; this family is facing financial and housing burdens of a crippling kind; this young person is coping with cancer. They come to the altar of God and receive the bread of life. They return to lives that are ordinary and humdrum and heroic...

In confession you hear what only the Almighty should hear. Like God, as they stumble out their sins and omissions, you hear the goodness that they are not aware of, and are humbled. Like God, you find them, as they do not find themselves, lovable, touchingly lovable.

John Farrell OP

21 | Protection

O God, our most mighty Protector,
safe in your tender care, let us hope.
Let us believe in your support, both
when we are young and when we are old.
Let us understand that when our
strength is from you, it is real
strength, but when it springs from
our own efforts, it is weakness.

St Augustine 354 – 430

22 | Purpose

You are needed where you are.
As in the heavens each and every star fills
    appointed space.
  So you fill that place where God has need.
Oh, do not doubt –
    your hand held out to help a friend,
    your love to warm an empty heart,
    even your smile to light the dark,
walk serene in grace;
you are in your needed place.

Elizabeth Searle Lamb

23 | Purpose

A prayer for the one who is left

Lord, the trouble about life just now is that I seem to have all the things that don't matter, and to have lost all the things which do matter.

I have life, I have enough money to live on, I have plenty to occupy me; but I am alone and sometimes I feel that nothing can make up for that.

Lord, compel me to see the meaning of my faith. Make me to realise that I have hope as well as a memory, and the unseen cloud of witnesses is around me, that you meant it when you said that you would be always with me. Make me realise that as long as you leave me here there is something I am meant to do, and in doing it help me to find the comfort and the courage that I need to go on.

Author unknown

24 | Purpose

Across the immensity of time and the disconcerting multiplicity of individuals one single operation is taking place: the annexation to Christ of his chosen; one single thing is being made: the Mystical Body of Christ...

Pierre Teilhard de Chardin 1881 – 1955

25 | Purpose

The great thing in this world is not so much where we are, but in what direction we are moving.

Anon.

26 | Reality

The source of most pain is in the conflict between the reality we would like to encounter and the reality in which we find ourselves, in our inability to shape reality to our own requirements. Yet the obdurate quality of reality, its refusal to be shaped by our demands on it, is a blessing, because it forces us out of the prison of our own conditioning, our own narrowness, and frees us from the grooves of our habitual thinking.

Gerard W. Hughes SJ

27 | Redemption

Through the experience of God's love shown them in Jesus, people are converted, changed, made capable of loving truly. By loving and serving others, Jesus gives them the capacity and power to love. This is the situation we meet throughout the gospels in the case of people whom Jesus meets and changes by meeting.

What is true of Jesus' earthly ministry and the people he met is still true. In opening ourselves to Jesus Christ in faith we find ourselves addressed by God's love and we find to our surprise a new and creative power operating in us, transforming us. Jesus breaks down the forces of evil which seek to dominate and destroy us. He breaks down our closed-in, imprisoning selfishness, removes our alienation, enables us to smile again, to open and give ourselves to our true centres and above all to God. He makes us truly free, sharers in his own sovereign freedom. This is Jesus' work of redemption. He is the redeeming, enabling, smile of God turned upon us.

Thomas A. Marsh

28 | Redundancy

Lord, have mercy on all who have been made redundant. Help them as they face the shock and disbelief, then the sadness of loss. Give them help for each day as it comes. May they keep the sense of worth that comes from knowing that they matter to you and to those who love them most. We pray for their parents, partners and children. Help them to bear the sadness and the difficult reactions of the one who has been hurt. Give them all courage for the present and hope for the future.

29 | Reflection

It would be a sad waste of the few short years we live if the bodily journey from birth to death was not matched by a journey inwards. For it is only there, deep within, that we will find God and our truest selves. It is only there that we will discover a true perspective on the purpose and meaning of our lives. But this will only come if we are quite ruthless in finding the time and space to live reflectively in the midst of a busy world.

Unless we do so, we wiii make a superficial journey through life and carry with us a sense of emptiness and waste.

Bishop John Crowley

30 Religion

What does the Lord require of you
　　but to do justice,
　　　　and to love kindness,
and to walk humbly with your God.

Micah 6:8b

October

1 | Religion

Do the Gospel deeds and you will know the Gospel truths. Religion is not learned, it is practised; the learning is in the doing but the doing is not a copying of anyone else's life but a living of one's own life.

R.E.C. Browne 1906 – 1975

2 | Religious experience

The true meaning of a religious experience does not lie in the transformation it effects in our lives, but in the fact that in it we have known God. That is what is lasting, even if our life remains a mixture of the divine and the human. That is what helps us to accept the drama of human life, which results from the very fact of the unending conflict in us between the divine and the human. It is indeed to the extent to which our experience has borne real fruit, to the extent to which our lives and our natures have undergone palpable, manifest change, that we can witness to the power of God. But that power goes far beyond our puny witness. What matters is not our experiences, but the fact that in them we have known the power of God's grace. That is a thing we do not forget, even if the day must come when the weaknesses, temptations and sins from which we had thought ourselves finally delivered reappear on the horizon; even if we must tirelessly battle on against our nature.

That is our task, to battle on, to hold our own against our inborn tendencies to strong or weak reactions, which we were given when we were given life itself, and which will be with us as long as we live. But the battle will not be the same as it was before. The faith born in us as a result of a concrete religious experience, survives even if we backslide. What is radically changed is the climate of our lives. Though our innate tendencies will remain with us, we shall on the other hand find it possible to break out of the vicious circles I have described, which constantly exacerbate those tendencies. Then if we still discover in ourselves, to our dismay, strong or weak natural reactions, far from being discouraged, we shall see them as opportunities for new deliverances.

Paul Tournier 1905 – 1986

3 Remembrance

Remember me when I am gone away,
    Gone far away into the silent land;
    When you can no more hold me by the hand,
Nor I half turn to go yet turning stay.
Remember me when no more day by day
    You tell me of our future that you planned:
    Only remember me; you understand
It will be late to counsel then or pray.
Yet if you should forget me for a while
    And afterward remember, do not grieve:
    For if the darkness and corruption leave
    A vestige of the thoughts that once I had,
Better by far you should forget and smile
    Than that you should remember and be sad.

Christina Rossetti 1830 – 1894

4 Respect

It is amazing and wonderful that the Creator treats each one of us as an individual person and with respect. He does not force us, although he may strongly and clearly offer to lead us. He presents each one of us throughout our lives with numerous choices of varying importance. Whenever we fail, he gives us more chances. If our key decisions, at least, are made with him in mind and with the wish not to offend him, then we shall gradually fulfil our destiny with his help. He enlists our cooperation throughout. There are times when he wishes us to be active; there are also periods when he expects us to be almost passive in his hands, for we have to learn in practice that we are dependent upon him. This can be painful, but when we have come through we shall see that the work was really his. All that we had to do was to accept him, turn fully towards him, and trust and love him. He gives and he does all the rest.

Jane Milward

5 | Resurrection

The resurrection is for Christians the supreme sign that God does indeed act in this world to bring life out of death, hope out of despair, victory out of defeat, and vindication to those who trust him. It is an invitation to live hopefully and to pray faithfully, because it shows us that just as we are free to 'do a new thing', so is God.

Archbishop John Habgood

6 | Sabbath

Father, I thank you for the precious gift of this Sabbath, and for the rest it brings to my body and spirit. I thank you for the opportunities it gives me to come closer to those I love and to those who worship with me. I thank you for this welcome break in the round of worldly occupations, for this chance of reading my own heart, of estimating more accurately how I stand towards you, and towards my own soul. On this day of calm and holiness I see my life more clearly and in its true perspective. My judgment of it comes nearer to yours. The things I thought were big now seem pitifully small; and what I thought was worthless or unimportant now seems filled with significance and meaning. I compare my pleasures and possessions to the knowledge of your truth and goodness and they fade into nothingness. Bless this clearer insight, this truer judgment. Give me the strength and integrity to go forward in joy, with this light which illuminates my being, into the coming week. Amen.

Forms of Prayer for Jewish Worship

7 Scripture

Fragments of scripture learned in happier days will be used by the Holy Spirit to supply help in time of need. These may be of any length, but are often quite short – a sentence, a phrase, even one or two words. To combat the shattering sense of disunity and disharmony that is a part of depression, how often I have cried to God in the words of Psalm 86:11 – 'Unite my heart to fear thy name!' – and known his healing touch! And I could not count the hours I have lived by the strength of the one word, 'Jesus!' It's a good idea to jot down helpful texts as you encounter them and to keep them ready for use in times of need.

Margaret Clarkson

8 Scripture

If, as the apostle Paul says, Christ is the power of God and the wisdom of God, then he who is ignorant of the scriptures is also ignorant of the power of God and

146

his wisdom; ignorance of the scriptures is ignorance of Christ.

St Jerome c. 342 – 420

9 | Self

The one important thing I have learnt over the years is the difference between taking one's work seriously and taking oneself seriously.

The first is imperative – the second disastrous.

Dame Margot Fonteyn 1919 – 1991

10 | Self-denial

True self-denial is the way in which we make room in our lives for the presence of God. We can do this in a number of ways: we can learn to become silent, listening to God; we can find solitude and become uncluttered in our desire for God; we can give him our attention, to be more deeply aware of how we need him; we can become obedient to his will, surrendering ourselves to his rule.

James Houston

11 | Self-knowledge

He who knows others is wise;
    He who knows himself is enlightened.

12 | Self-sufficiency

I know that (God) is far more willing to do things for us than we are to ask him. And that is the great mystery –

147

why, knowing what we do about God's power and God's willingness to help, why we keep on struggling ourselves... trying to work out things our own way, when he could save us all the anxiety, do it better and easier.

I believe our pretended, pathetic self-sufficiency saddens God. He longs to help us, but we won't let him. We refuse to ask him.

Peter Marshall 1902 – 1949

13 | Self-worth

Only God can give us the sense of our own preciousness and ultimate significance. Only in a life rooted deeply in prayer, where we can live contentedly hidden in Christ and, there, accept the martyrdom of obscurity, will our aching and dissatisfaction cease and our disease give way to restful contentment.

Ronald Rolheiser OMI

14 | Separation and divorce

This death (the death of a relationship) was for me the complete destruction of a first life. Everything on which I had built, all that I had hoped for, believed, wanted, was destroyed. The experience is probably similar to that of the death of someone one loves very much. Except that in the story of a marriage and a separation the element of guilt necessarily plays a greater part and the awareness of having forgotten something, neglected it and got it irrevocably wrong cannot be assuaged by any form of belief in fate. It took me three years, not to come to terms with it, but to overcome the suicidal fantasies which constantly dogged me. Wanting to die was my only hope, my only thought. In this situation I once went into one of those old Gothic churches on a journey through Belgium. The expression 'pray' now seems to me to be wrong. I was one lonely cry. I cried for help, and behind it I could imagine two things: that my husband would come back to me, or that I would die and this constant torture would finally cease. In this church, submerged in my cry, a saying from the Bible occurred to me, 'Let my grace be enough for you.'

Dorothy Sölle

15 | Separation and divorce

Prayer for me is a journey, a relationship with God, a discovery. It is exciting. Often nothing at all seems to happen and I try to find excuses to wriggle out of it. However, I just know I cannot live without it. I wrestle with God, run away from him, long and hunger enormously for him. In prayer I ask for the courage to open my heart to him and I ask him to make me brave enough to want to see like Bartimaeus.

I gasp breathlessly as I meet in prayer God in anguish. In the garden of Gethsemane I fall in love with the God who so painfully knows his own humanity. This God who knows his need of friends and suffers the agonies of loneliness, rejection and fear is one I can identify with, for I know he is the real God and the only one I can adore. I meet him in Gethsemane as the one who refused to short-circuit his human suffering and I know him as the Lover who embraces his beloved. He leads me from the depths of the grave of spiritual death, divorce and a broken family to start slowly to trust again. It is when I look at the lives of the people around me – often fellow divorcees – who have also wept, sweated blood and somehow crawled out of their prisons that I realise the life of each one of us is 'holy ground' where God is mysteriously wiping away our fears, mending the rubble of our broken lives and leading us from darkness to light. It is then that I want to sing like Mary, 'My soul magnifies the Lord, my spirit rejoices in God my Saviour', for then I know he does not abandon us. Although he might lead us to the grave, he does indeed bring us back.

Tessa Sheaf

16 Service

I don't know what your destiny will be, but one thing I know, the only ones among you who will be really happy are those who have sought and found how to serve.

Albert Schweitzer 1875 – 1965

17 Service

Make us worthy, Lord, to serve our fellow men throughout the world who live and die in poverty and hunger.

Give them through our hands this day their daily bread, and by our understanding love, give peace and joy.

Mother Teresa of Calcutta

18 Service

A service which involves emptying oneself and working for the good of others is at the very heart of the Christian vocation. The follower of Christ does not seek power and riches in order to manipulate other human beings and beggar the earth. Rather he hears the call, 'if anyone wants to be a follower of mine, let him renounce himself and take up his cross every day and follow me.'

Sean McDonagh SSC

19 | Sickness

At the end of the day what really matters is not that we should all get better and live happily ever after, as in some unreal fairy tale. What alone is important is that God's will may be done, and his Kingdom come, in the circumstances of this experience, this sickness, this action.

Michael Mayne

20 | Silence

O Lord, the Scripture says
'there is a time for silence and a time for speech.'
Saviour, teach me the silence of humility,
the silence of wisdom,
the silence of love,
the silence of perfection,
the silence that speaks without words,
the silence of faith.

Lord, teach me to silence my own heart that I may listen to the gentle movement of the Holy Spirit within me and sense the depths which are of God.

Prayer from Frankfurt, 16th c.

21 | Silence

We need silence to be able to touch souls. The essential thing is not what we say but what God says to us and through us.

Karl Rahner SJ 1904 – 1984

22 | Silence

We need to recover oases of silence within the rhyme and reason of our active life, for it is in silence that we meet God face to face.

Max Picard

23 | Silence

Silence is the language of God;
  it is also the language of the heart.

Swami Sivananda

24 | Silence

God speaks in silences,
  and only those who are quiet of heart
    can hear what he says.

Thomas H. Green SJ

25 | Silence

The more we listen to the silence within,
  the more we shall begin to hear
    the silence in other people,
to hear the things they do not say
    or cannot put into words.

James Roose-Evans

26 | Sin

The measure in which we fail to love is the measure in which we sin. You can list as many sins as you like, but they are only sins if they are acts of non-love.

Pierre Riches

27 | Sin

To confess our sins is to accuse ourselves of them: quite a different thing from merely telling them. We may tell our sins by way of boast, we may tell them to intimate friends for the sake of sympathy; but to confess them is to acknowledge their guilt, to recognise them as an injury to another; to own to our action in the matter and yet be willing to repudiate it. For it is not more contrary to the essence of true confession to deny our deed than to defend it; in the former case we try, fruitlessly, to obliterate the past; in the latter we endeavour to carry over the past into the future and to crystallise the attitude in such a way that our soul is changed in the telling of it. What is done in the external and material order can never be undone or altered; but the spiritual act, which is in the soul itself, is never really past, and can be qualified, and transformed, like all living things, by the infusion of new elements. Thus do we modify our sin in the telling of it, and become again pleasing instead of displeasing to the one against whom we have sinned. And this is done, not by making out an act to be other than it was, but, on the contrary, by taking towards it the attitude prescribed by truth and justice.

Maude Petre 1863 – 1942

28 Sin

Sin is always loving badly, or not loving at all. Redemption is Jesus Christ restoring to the world the full weight of love – of which man robbed it through his sin.

Michel Quoist

29 Social concern

Any religion which professes to be concerned about the souls of men and is not concerned about the social and economic conditions that can scar the soul, is a spiritually moribund religion only waiting for the day to be buried.

Martin Luther King 1929 – 1968

30 Social concern

To claim to be a Christian or a Jew who loves God and neighbour and not to take an active part in the formation of just social policies affecting those neighbours would seem to deny complete fulfilment of one's faith.

Reubin Askew

31 Solitude

Come now, little man,
turn aside for a while from your daily employment,
escape for a moment from the tumult of your thoughts.
Put aside your weighty cares,
let your burdensome distractions wait,
free yourself awhile for God
and rest awhile in him.

Enter the inner chamber of your soul,
    shut out everything except God
    and that which can help you in seeking him,
    and when you have shut the door, seek him.

St Anselm c. 1033 – 1109

November

1 | Solitude

In the lonely place Jesus finds the courage to follow God's will and not his own; to speak God's words and not his own; to do God's work and not his own. He reminds us constantly: 'I can do nothing by myself... my aim is to do not my own will, but the will of him who sent me' (John 5:30), and again, 'The words I say to you I do not speak as from myself: it is the Father, living in me, who is doing this work' (John 14:10). It is in the lonely place where Jesus enters into intimacy with the Father that his ministry is born. Somewhere we know that without a lonely place our lives are in danger. Somewhere we know that without silence words lose their meaning, that without listening speaking no longer heals, that without distance closeness cannot cure. Somewhere actions quickly become empty gestures. The careful balance between silence and words, withdrawal and involvement, distance and closeness, solitude and community forms the basis of the Christian life.

Henri Nouwen

2 | Solitude

When from our better selves we have too long
   Been parted by the hurrying world, and droop,
Sick of its business, of its pleasures tired,
   How gracious, how benign, is solitude.

William Wordsworth 1770 – 1850

3 | Solitude

As soon as a man is fully disposed to be alone with God, he is alone with God no matter where he may be – in the country, the monastery, the woods or the city.

156

The lightning flashes from east to west, illuminating the whole horizon and striking where it pleases and at the same instant the infinite liberty of God flashes in the depths of that man's soul, and he is illumined. At that moment he sees that though he seems to be in the middle of his journey, he has already arrived at the end. For the life of grace on earth is the beginning of the life of glory. Although he is a traveller in time, he has opened his eyes, for a moment, in eternity.

Thomas Merton 1915 – 1968

4 | Spirituality

Countless as are the needs of the present world, none is greater than its need of spiritual power, something to lift man above the sordidness of materialism; something to cause him to look out, not in; up, not down; to help him to turn the defeat of his selfish purposes into victorious living for others.

John D. Rockefeller Jr. 1874 – 1960

5 | Spirituality

Great men are they who see that the spiritual is stronger than any material force; that thoughts rule the world.

Ralph Waldo Emerson 1803 – 1882

6 | Spirituality

... stopped by the touch of a sick woman, he
turned about –
he who conquered death
he who defeated Satan

he whom all the legions of hell cannot stop
he who is King of kings.

He stopped just because a sick and nameless woman touched the hem of his garment.
We need to touch him – O how much we need to touch him!
(...) because when we are not in touch, there is no vitality in our spiritual life.

Peter Marshall 1902 – 1949

7 | Stillness

If you can remain inwardly 'still' when all around you is raging, then your stillness can be used by God, as a centrepoint through which he can radiate, as it were, rays of calmness and quietude so that the storm around you will slowly and gently die away, enabling his love and his calm to penetrate deep into the hearts of those whose minds and spirits are not at rest.

To be such a centrepoint, whether you are blind, deaf, dumb, or handicapped in any way, is to be a means by which God can transform *you* into a special envoy in his heavenly kingdom. Never let any physical or mental handicap deter you from this, for those of you who are in this position have an especial role to play in helping those who are not as yourselves.

Patricia M. Vardigans

8 | Stillness

Let us, then, labour for an inward stillness –
An inward stillness and an inward healing;
That perfect silence where the lips and heart
Are still, and we no longer entertain

Our own imperfect thoughts and vain opinions,
But God alone speaks in us, and we wait
In singleness of heart, that we may know
His will, and in silence of our spirits,
That we may do his will and do that only.

Henry Wadsworth Longfellow 1807– 1882

9 | Strength

Where do you get the strength to go on, when you have
used up all your own strength? Where do you turn for
patience when you have run out of patience, when you
have been more patient for more years than anyone
should be asked to be, and the end is nowhere in sight?
I believe that God gives us strength and patience and
hope, renewing our spiritual resources when they run
dry. How else do sick people manage to find more
strength and more good humour over the course of
prolonged illness than any one person could possibly
have, unless God was constantly replenishing their souls?
How else do widows find the courage to pick up the
pieces of their lives and go out to face the world alone,
when, on the day of their husband's funeral, they did
not have that courage? How else do the parents of a
retarded or brain-damaged youngster wake up every
morning and turn again to their responsibilities, unless
they are able to lean on God when they grow weak?

We don't have to beg or bribe God to give us strength
or hope or patience. We need only turn to him, admit
that we can't do this on our own, and understand that
bravely bearing up under long-term illness is one of the
most human, and one of the most godly, things we can
ever do. One of the things that constantly reassures me
that God is real, and not just an idea that religious
leaders made up, is the fact that people who pray for
strength, hope and courage so often find resources of

strength, hope and courage that they did not have before they prayed.

Harold S. Kushner

10 | Strength

Relieve and comfort, O Lord,
    all the persecuted and afflicted;
speak peace to troubled consciences;
    strengthen the weak;
confirm the strong;
    instruct the ignorant;
deliver the oppressed from him that spoilest him;
    relieve the needy that hath no helper;
and bring us all, by the waters of comfort
    and in the ways of righteousness,
to thy kingdom of rest and glory;
    through Jesus Christ our Lord.

Bishop Jeremy Taylor 1613 – 1667

11 | Stress

Blessed be Jesus who is always near in times of stress.
Even when we cannot feel his presence he is close.

Margery Kempe c. 1373 – 1433

12 | Success

To laugh often and love much
To win the respect of intelligent persons
    and the affection of children
To learn the approbation of honest critics
    and endure the betrayal of false friends

To appreciate beauty
   To find the best in others
      To give one's self
To leave the world a bit better,
   whether by a healthy child,
      a garden patch or
         a redeemed social condition
To have played and laughed with enthusiasm
      and sung with exultation
To know even one life has breathed easier
      because you have lived –
This is to have succeeded.

Ralph Waldo Emerson 1803 – 1882

13 | Suffering

In sorrow and suffering,
   go straight to God with confidence,
      and you will be strengthened,
         enlightened and instructed.

St John of the Cross 1542 – 1591

14 | Suffering

... it is the nature of human privations and sufferings of all kinds to feel like dead-ends. But human suffering, the more of a dead-end it feels like, the more is it an invitation to join in Christ's sufferings, and in him to help bring life and light and healing and liberty to mankind. So the cruelly destructive and negative nature of suffering can be seen if only in a glass very darkly, as charged with positive and creative possibilities. Of course it isn't calculable. It's a mystery, which means it's too real for precise definition.

H.A. Williams

15 | Suffering

When I cry out, 'Why me?'
 what I am really asking is:
  'What can I become or what can I do for others
   because of my experience of suffering?'

Frank Maier

16 | Suffering .

Sickness, pain and tragedy belong among those realities in life which we first simply have to accept as beyond our understanding, yet which we grasp more clearly with the passage of time. In respect of all mysteries, along with whatever degree of limited apprehension we may have in any particular case there goes the concomitant intuition that we will never understand completely. To acknowledge suffering as a mystery prevents us from making our intellectual difficulties and mental agonies the sole guidelines to any conclusions we might reach about its origin and meaning.

Eric Doyle OFM 1938 – 1986

17 | Suffering

O God,
the refuge of the poor,
the strength of those who toil,
and the comforter of all who sorrow,
we commend to your mercy the unfortunate
and needy in whatever land they may be.
You alone know the number and extent
of their sufferings and trials.
Look down, Father of Mercies,

at those unhappy families suffering
from war and slaughter, from hunger and disease,
and other severe trials.
Spare them, O Lord, for it is truly a time for mercy.

St Peter Canisius 1521 – 1597

18 | Suffering

We do well to remember that Christianity did not invent
suffering. Suffering was already in the world since time
began. Christianity worked out a creative way of hand-
ling it: to fight against it when it is unnecessary, but to
accept it lovingly when it is the way to do Christ's will.
Christianity thus gave a meaning to suffering. This meaning is not that suffering is good in itself but that, in
God's providence, it is an opportunity to love – the
supreme test in many instances.

John Dalrymple 1928 – 1985

19 | Suffering

This is important to realise that though God came to us
at a certain point in history, that Jesus was crucified on a
particular Friday, his entry is indeed timeless, and when
a man or woman made in God's image is suffering, God
is suffering.

Dom Edmund Jones OSB

20 | Suffering

It is in suffering that we discover the things that matter;
in sorrow we discover ourselves.

Mary Craig

21 | Suffering

... the *fiat* God asks of us when we suffer is not the *fiat* of insensibility, but of suffering. When our heart is torn and continues to be so, we must give it to him as it is. Later, when peace returns, we will give it to him at peace. What he wants is for us to give ourselves to him as we are. If there is anything to be put right he will do that, because we shall have handed ourselves over completely to him.

A Carthusian

22 | Thanksgiving

Let us give thanks this moment: -
for the sturdy fact of God's continuing love,
for mercies which go before us
and follow after us,
for those free gifts
which cost God so much.

Let us give thanks:
for memory and expectation,
for the good that we have known
and know today in Jesus Christ,
for the Spirit's brooding presence
in our nights and in our days.

Let us give thanks:
for pleasures which comfort
and pains which force our growth
and keep us at the Shepherd's side,
for deep meanings revealed
and mysteries, mercifully concealed,
for the image of God within us,
the capacity to inquire and adore.

Let us give thanks for one another,
for just being together,
for differences which complement and complete,
for gifts which enrich
and disagreements which challenge,
for our oneness in Christ.

Let us give thanks for melody and mirth,
for rhythm and beat,
for the repeated and the common,
for the ever-unfolding,
and for senses with which to respond.

And let us give thanks for Someone to thank.

23 | Thanksgiving

Even in the troubled days of our life we should still
  praise him.
Thank the Lord for saving us, for calling us.
Thank the Lord that in the midst of difficult times we are
  still alive.
Thank the Lord for bestowing upon us all kinds of
  spiritual blessings.
Thank the Lord for bestowing upon us hope and trust
  in him.
Thank the Lord for bestowing upon us comfort and joy.
Thank the Lord for bestowing upon us the strength to
  endure hardship.
Thank the Lord that he has not treated us according to
  our sins.
Thank the Lord for his promise to bestow on us a
  heavenly eternal home, a kingdom that can never be
  shaken, and incomparable, everlasting glory.

Be thankful that by the grace of our Lord Jesus Christ we
can go calmly and without fear into the presence of

God, we can receive forgiveness and the blessing of his mercy, his help and protection at all times.

If we have truly learned to 'give thanks in all circumstances' then even in times of trouble we will never feel the slightest hardship.

Wang Mingdao

24 | Time

It is far from easy to decide how to balance all the various demands upon our limited time, so that it becomes a harmonious whole, a living, dramatised psalm of praise to the glory of our God. It is so easy to use time disproportionately... We need to pray for ourselves and for each other, as Paul did, that we may 'discern what is important.'

Michael Griffiths

25 | Time

At the beginning of the week, as I have looked ahead to what I was supposed to be doing, where I was supposed to be going, I have often found myself asking, 'Lord, how on earth am I actually going to make it?' That sense of panic is already present as you wonder just how you are going to get through a particular set of circumstances, a particular week, even a particular day. But then, as we look back, we find that we did actually get through it! But we would have to add, 'with God's grace'.

Bishop David Hope

26 | Tolerance

The most lovable quality any human being can possess is tolerance. It is the vision that enables one to see things from another's viewpoint. It is the generosity that concedes to others the right to their own opinions and peculiarities. It is the bigness that enables us to let people be happy in their own way instead of our way.

27 | Tolerance

God of all tolerance
and patience,
in your great and full mercy
you are compassionate.

> You take faults away,
> constantly overlook times of ignorance,
> wait many years when we show no fear of you.
> You do not treat us as our sins deserve
> nor does your wrath last for ever.

God of all goodness and grace,
in Christ Jesus our Saviour
your kindness and generosity
dawns in love for all mankind.

I will praise you as long as I live,
I will sing to you my God all my life.
Every day will I thank you,
I will praise you for ever and ever.

Lancelot Andrewes 1555 – 1626

28 Trinity

We are enclosed in the Father, and we are enclosed in
the Son, and we are enclosed in the Holy Ghost. And
the Father is enclosed in us, and the Son is enclosed in
us, and the Holy Ghost is enclosed in us: Almightiness,
All Wisdom, All Goodness: one God, one Lord.

Julian of Norwich c.1342 – after 1413

29 Trinity

God Who is Father
Be merciful to us.
God Who is Son
Be Brother to us.
God Who is Spirit
Be Love to us.
God Who is One
Unite us who are many.
God Who is Three
Watch over each one of us.
God Who is Truth
Blot out our lies.
God Who is Life
Live on in all of us.
God the Incomprehensible
Make us understand.
God the Unutterable
Say but the word.
God the Unmeasurable
Widen our vision.
God the Unchangeable
Make us our true selves.
God Ancient of everlasting days
Be near us this moment.
God of Light Inaccessible

Help us to see.
God of Fire All-Consuming
Warm our cold hearts.
God of Air All-Pervading
Be in each one of us.
God of Water All-Cleansing
Wash out our guilt.
God of Earth All-Sustaining
Inspire us to share.
God the All-Holy
Teach us your ways.
God the All-Merciful
Make us kind to each other.
God the All-Powerful
Be strength in our weakness.
God the Transcendent
Draw closer to us.
God the Eternal
Take care of our time.
God the Creator
Watch over the world.
God of the Universe
Bless all you have made. Amen.

Eric Doyle OFM 1938 – 1986

30 | Troubled times

God is our refuge and our strength,
      a very present help in trouble.

Psalm 46:1

December

1 | Troubled times

Lord you are a present help in trouble.
Come revive
Redeem
Restore
In our darkness come as light
In our sadness come as joy
In our troubles come as peace
In our weakness come as strength
Come Lord to our aid
Revive
Redeem
Restore us

O Lord
   Open our eyes to your presence
   Open our minds to your grace
   Open our lips to your praises
   Open our hearts to your love
   Open our lives to your healing
   And be found among us.

David Adam

2 | Trust

You can never trust God too much.
Why is it that some people do not bear fruit?
It is because they have no trust
either in God or in themselves.

Meister Eckhart c. 1260 – 1327

3 | Trust

Written for someone in distress over a loved one's illness

When you sit with your sorrow; with your grief
Do not let them become a torrent wherein you can
    easily drown
But rest, quietly, in the warmth and Love of Christ who
    holds you

He holds you – his child

Each child of his is special to him

When we come to him in our grief
He opens his arms to receive us
No matter how unworthy we feel
He is there, ready to welcome us his special child

Rest quietly in his loving
He will hold you tenderly as a mother holds her child
He will hold you gently as a treasured possession
You are a treasure to him because you have come
    to him

Rest quietly in his love
Let his Compassion and Mercy o'ershadow you;
    hold you
Tell him your troubles
He will listen
In the stillness; in the silence he listens to each and
    every heart
He knows our every need
Speak with him
Listen in the Silence as you rest in him
And he will surely speak
Filling you – his child – with the richness of his Love
Do not be afraid

Succumb to him
He will not let you fall
Weep with him as he surely weeps with you
Have faith – Have trust
Become a child again
With child-like faith; with child-like trust
Come to him
His arms are ever open

Judith Ann Pounder

4 | Trust

With all my heart and soul, O God, I thank you that in all the changes and chances of this mortal life I can look up to you and cheerfully resign my will to yours. I have trusted you, O Father, with myself. My soul is in your hand, which I truly believe you will preserve from all evil – my body and all that belongs to it are of much less value. I do therefore, with as great a sense of security as satisfaction, trust all I have to you.

Thomas Wilson 1663 – 1755

5 | Trust

Trust is the greatest joy in our relationship with God. Whoever trusts in God has already covered the hardest part of the journey...

God, you are my God, I can count on you.

Carlo Carretto

6 | Trust

Be still, my soul: the Lord is on thy side;
 Bear patiently the cross of grief or pain;
Leave to thy God to order and provide;
 In every change he faithful will remain.
Be still, my soul: thy best, thy heavenly Friend
Through thorny ways leads to a joyful end.

Be still, my soul: thy God doth undertake
 To guide the future as he has the past.
Thy hope, thy confidence let nothing shake;
 All now mysterious shall be bright at last,
Be still, my soul: the waves and winds still know
His voice who ruled them while he dwelt below.

Be still, my soul: when dearest friends depart,
 And all is darkened in the vale of tears,
Then shalt thou better know his love, his heart,
 Who comes to soothe thy sorrow and thy fears.
Be still, my soul: thy Jesus can repay,
From his own fullness, all he takes away.

Be still, my soul: the hour is hastening on
 When we shall be for ever with the Lord,
When disappointment, grief and fear are gone,
 Sorrow forgot, love's purest joys restored.
Be still, my soul: when change and tears are past,
All safe and blessed we shall meet at last.

Katherina von Schlegel 1697 – ?

7 | Trust

This trust Jesus showed is tied up with the intimate
knowledge he had of his disciples. He knew their
strengths and weaknesses; he knew just how unreliable

173

they were; and yet taking all this into consideration, he trusted them with his life and his work. And he treats us likewise.

Michael Hollings

8 | Trust

Whenever you feel confused, bewildered, disillusioned, frightened, be childlike in your trust in God, present and beckoning you in the chaos. In trusting with your heart, it is as though you put your hand in his and let him lead you.

Gerard W. Hughes SJ

9 | Trust

Be happy to feel that you cannot control your life, that there is so much in you that you seem unable to cope with. Trust yourself to him, take each moment as it comes, for each moment holds him. Let him have the say, let him take charge, even though you are left feeling no one is in charge.

Ruth Burrows

10 | Truth

This is TRUTH:
    The divine life planted in the hearts of men,
life linked to life through all the centuries.
    A living growth that grows by living,
and as it lives unfolds
the secret knowledge of the life of Christ.
    Life calling to life across the centuries
ever finding fresh answers,

ever dropping fresh sparks of life
 into the hearts that live.

Edward Thring 1821 – 1887

11 | Unemployment

Father, I pray for those who have no paid employment
and who have no colleagues, that they may not despair
but may find other ways of working for the well-being
of society and may find fellowship in common enter-
prise. Bless those whose days of retirement have separated them from colleagues and give them a sense of
their continuing worth as your children. Enlarge our
experience of community life that we may see each
other as fellow workers in your wider kingdom, because we all belong to one another in Christ.

12 | Unity

When we say that unity must be in truth and holiness
we are saying that the secret of coming nearer to one
another is that we should all of us become nearer to
Christ. He welcomes us to an amazing nearness to
himself; that is the secret if only we will receive his
welcome.

Think how Christ welcomed you in your baptism and
your confirmation. Think how he welcomes you in the
Blessed Sacrament with the scarcely believable intimacy
of his real presence. Think how he welcomes you in
absolution when he washes your sins from you just as
he washed the feet of the apostles in the upper room.
Think how he welcomes you as you find him and are
near to him in the holy scriptures. It is an intimacy so
aweful, so humbling. And for all our sins and failings he

welcomes us already into fellowship with Blessed Mary and the saints in heaven as we join our prayers and our praises with theirs in the Communion of Saints.

But what does this welcome demand of us? What is the practical test of its validity? We know the answer. It is that we should actually become Christlike: in humility, in generosity, in courage, in self-forgetfulness. And that is why Christ's welcome to us always includes the privilege of suffering with him, if he wills it; of having a little share in his Passion, of knowing that Calvary is a reality, not only a name. But when we accept his welcome to all that, we find the deep joy that marks the life of a Christian. We hear Jesus saying to us, 'These things have I said to you, that my joy may be in you and that your joy may be full.'

Archbishop Michael Ramsey 1904 – 1988
preaching in Westminster Cathedral 1968

13 | Values

... get your scale of values right and whatever job you are called to, it will help your soul to grow towards God.

Evelyn Underhill 1875 – 1941

14 | Virtue

Love means to love that which is unlovable,
    or it is no virtue at all;
forgiving means to pardon the unpardonable,
    or it is no virtue at all;
faith means believing the unbelievable,
    or it is no virtue at all.
And to hope means hoping when things are hopeless,
    or it is no virtue at all.

G.K. Chesterton 1874 – 1936

176

15 | Vocation

... the first step in Abraham's pilgrimage of faith was one of blind obedience. He had God's promise and that was enough. When the call came, he obeyed it. He did not demand to have everything explained to him first so that he could then make up his mind whether he would follow God's call or not. Knowing it was God's call, he obeyed it simply because it was God's call. That's what it means to follow God. If it had been the call of a mere human being, he would have been wise to demand to know and understand all the details before he decided whether to follow it. But he couldn't treat God that way.

David Gooding

16 | Vulnerability

And so we must begin to live again,
We of the damaged bodies
And assaulted minds.
Starting from scratch with the rubble of our lives
And picking up the dust
Of dreams once dreamt.

And we stand there, naked in our vulnerability,
Proud of starting over, fighting back,
But full of weak humility
At the awesomeness of the task.

We, without a future,
Safe, defined, delivered
Now salute you, God.
Knowing that nothing is safe,
Secure, inviolable here.
Except you,
And even that eludes our minds at times.

And we hate you
As we love you,
And our anger is as strong
As our pain,
Our grief is deep as oceans,
And our need as great as mountains.

So, as we take our first few steps forward
Into the abyss of the future,
We would pray for
Courage to go places for the first time
And just be there.
Courage to become what we have
Not been before
And accept it,
And bravery to look deep
Within our souls to find
New ways.

We did not want it easy, God,
But we did not contemplate
That it would be quite this hard,
This long, this lonely.

So, if we are to be turned inside out,
And upside down,
With even our pockets shaken,
Just to check what's rattling
And left behind,
We pray that you will keep faith with us,
And we with you,
Holding our hands as we weep,
Giving us strength to continue,
And showing us beacons
Along the way
To becoming new.

We are not fighting you, God,
Even if it feels like it,
But we need your help and company,
As we struggle on.
Fighting back
And starting over.

Anna McKenzie

17 | Weakness

If I should decide to boast,
I should not be made to look foolish,
because I should only be speaking the truth;
but I am not going to,
in case anyone should begin to think I am better than
he can actually see and hear me to be.

In view of the extraordinary nature of these
    revelations,
to stop me from getting too proud I was given a
thorn in the flesh, an Angel of Satan to beat me
and stop me from getting too proud!
About this thing, I have pleaded with the Lord
three times for it to leave me, but he has said,
'My grace is enough for you;
my power is at its best in weakness'.
So I shall be very happy to make my weknesses
my special boast so that the power of Christ
may stay over me,
and that is why I am content with my weaknesses,
and with insults, hardships, persecutions,
and the agonies I go through for Christ's sake.
For it is when I am weak that I am strong.

2 Corinthians 12:6 – 10

18 | Weakness

In God's topsy-turvy approach to power, he takes weak, scarred, scared, struggling, failing and ineffective people and accomplishes his mighty work with such miserably inadequate tools.

Robert Girard

19 | Why?

'My God, my Father, why?'
That was thy piteous cry,
Sweet Lord, on Calvary.

In all perplexity,
Echoing agelessly,
Cometh that cry to me;

When I must stand and see
Some one apparently
Suffering uselessly;

Or worse than any pain
Look upon a life insane
Where death would seem a gain;

'Tis then thy questioning cry,
'My God, my Father, why?'
Comforteth me greatly.

If thou could'st question so,
I can through darkness go,
Contented not to know.

Yea, I can also see
How life's dark night may be
Love's opportunity.

Father Andrew

20 | Why?

Why should this happen to you? they say.
Why should this happen to you?
Why should life come to a standstill,
With no hope of dreams to survey?
Nothing to look for but pain or despair.
How can you live life this way?

The answer is simple and clear in my mind.
For the compensations are great,
And far outweigh the traumas of life
Which avalanche daily, combined
To precipitate pain and despair.
So where is the secret confined?

The secret lies in discovering worth,
Through others' reactions and feelings;
Through caring and sharing and healing.
One is learning of love since the moment of birth,
And the mind can respond where the body cannot
To find God's peace on this earth.

Liz Selby

21 | Will of God

Many classical writers see it as a sign of progress in the
spiritual life if, more and more, we put our own will and
desires behind us and accept what life brings as the will
of God. This is not to be confused with quietism, where

the person simply does nothing but accept life as it comes. The doctrine of acceptance of the divine will means that the individual constantly struggles to find God in whatever happens. The masters of the spiritual life call for very active acceptance of the divine will. This requires that the individual strive to do the best with whatever happens, and accept the vicissitudes of life and even the injustices which arise from human malice as part of the road to holiness.

_ *Benedict Groeschel CFR*

22 | Will of God

There is a world of difference between identifying my interests with God's (which is genuine holiness) and identifying God's interest with my own (which is the ultimate in vanity). Yet how subtle this difference is, and how easily we confuse the two in our lives.

Thomas H. Green SJ

23 | Will of God

If the will of God is that you should accept this or that interruption, and you accept them with gladness, then a day which might seem tempestuous is really filled with plan and peace and order; for where the will of God is there is God's presence and God's peace, and where that will is obeyed there is pattern and harmony. In his will is your peace.

Archbishop Michael Ramsey 1904 – 1988

December 24

What can I give him
Poor as I am?
If I were a shepherd
I would bring a lamb;
If I were a rich man
I would do my part;
Yet what can I give him –
Give my heart.

Christina Rossetti 1830 – 1894

December 25

... And is it true? And is it true?
This most tremendous tale of all,
Seen in a stained-glass window's hue,
A baby in an ox's stall?
The Maker of the stars and sea
Become a child on earth for me?

And is it true? For if it is,
No loving fingers tying strings
Around those tissued fripperies,
The sweet and silly Christmas things,
Bath salts and inexpensive scent
And hideous tie so kindly meant,

No love that in a family dwells,
No carolling in frosty air,
Nor all the steeple-shaking bells
Can with this simple truth compare –
That God was man in Palestine
And lives today in bread and wine.

Sir John Betjeman 1906 – 1984

26 Will of God

Lord let me come near this year,
And see and hear and sing
The mystery of God's self-emptying.

God's will, it is no grandiose thing
It is the little service that we bring
The open eye, the open ear –
To see – to hear
The insignificant and small
The heart of love to care, to share
A brother's need
That smile that takes the strife from dreary daily life.

God's will
It is the light of love, warmth
That lets the flower of faith
From tiny seed – tight bud – burst forth
Glorious in its simplicity.
There as a babe he lies – and cries
This tiny thing
Sent by the will of God
To let men know by way of manger and of cross
God gives – Emptying himself upon the earth.

Man grasps and makes a name – seeks fame.
God gives himself away and takes the lowest place.
Takes on himself the helplessness that every love must
    know.
God's will for men? Self-emptying.
Pouring out all their love.
And to bestow
Healing of heart and mind... Sight to the blind.
Let me come near this coming year
To see and hear and sing,
The mystery of God's self-emptying.

A nun of Burnham Abbey

27 | Wonder

Wonder is the opposite of cynicism and boredom; it indicates that a person has heightened aliveness, is interested, expectant, responsive. It is essentially an 'opening' attitude... an awareness that there is more to life than one has fathomed, an experience of new vistas of life to be explored as well as new profundities to be plumbed.

Rollo May

28 | Wonder

Socrates' statement that wonder is the beginning of all wisdom is true not only for wisdom but for the religious experience. One who has never been bewildered, who has never looked upon life and his own experience as phenomena which require answers and yet, paradoxically, for which the only answers are new questions, can hardly understand what religious experience is.

Erich Fromm

29 | Work

If we are to remain spiritually alive we need determination and skill to train ourselves to be flexible, that is, to turn from work to prayer and back again without the work suffering from lack of concentration or the prayer becoming mechanical. It is not that the Christian is to leave people and the world to pray and be holy; he is to be holy wherever he is in the noise and disturbance of modern conditions.

R.E.C. Browne 1906 – 1975

30 | Youth

O God our Father, we pray for our young people growing up in an unstable and confusing world. Show them that your ways give more meaning to life than the ways of the world and that following you is better than chasing after selfish goals. Help them to take failure not as a measure of their worth but as a chance for a new start. Give them strength to hold their faith in you and to keep alive their joy in your creation; through Jesus Christ our Lord.

Episcopal Church USA

31 | Youth

Father, we pray for young people growing up in a difficult and dangerous world.

We pray for those who are unemployed, who have not worked since they left school and have never earned their own money.

We pray for those who are taking their first steps in their skill, trade or profession.

We pray for those who feel they have no support from the adults around them and who grow resentful at what they see to be their indifference.

We pray for those who are caught up in violence either giving it or receiving it.

We pray for those who are morally confused and uncertain of what is right or wrong.

We pray for young Christians as they strive to live out their faith in an unsympathetic world.

Father, you are head of all the family. Hear our prayers in Jesus' name.

Index of Authors

187

Titles

Abandonment
Achievement
Action
Adversity
Availability

Baptism
Belief
Bereavement
Brokenness
Burdens

Change
Charter of belief
Choices
Chosen people
Christianity
Christ-like
Church
Comfort
Commitment
Companions
Compassion
Confidence
Contentment
Conversion
Courage
Crucifix

Death
Defeat
Desire
Difficulties
Discipleship
Discouragement
Dying

Easter
Empathy
Encouragement
End of the world
Eternal life

Eucharist
Experience

Faith
Fallibility
Farewell
Fear
Fidelity
Forgiveness
Frailty
Friendship
Future

Gentleness
Gift of life
Giving
God
God's action
God's presence
Gospel
Grace
Gratitude
Growth
Guidance
Guilt

Handicapped
Happiness
Heaven
Hell
Holiness
Holy Spirit
Hope
Humanity
Humility

Ideals
If ...
Inadequacy
Individuality
Integrity
Intercessions

Jesus Christ
Jesus Christ's disciples
Jesus Christ's presence
Jesus Christ's way

Joy
Kindness
Knowledge

Lent
Life
Listening
Loneliness
Love
Love of God
Love's demands
Love's eternity
Love's importance
Love's meaning
Love's strength

Marriage
Marriage anniversary
Mary
Meaning
Meeting God
Mental prayer
Mercy
Missionaries
Morning prayer

Nature
Need
Night prayer

Obedience
Old age
Others

Pain
Parenting
Patience

Peace
People of God
Perfection
Perspective
Pity
Poverty
Praise
Prayer
Prayer - a necessity
Prayer and contemplation
Prayer as gift
Prayer of attention
Prayer of Jesus
Prayer, the practice
Prayer unceasing
Prayer's effects
Prayer's language
Prayer's meaning
Present moment
Priesthood
Protection
Purpose

Reality
Redemption
Redundancy
Reflection
Religion
Religious experience
Remembrance
Respect
Resurrection

Sabbath
Scripture
Self
Self-denial
Self-knowledge
Self-sufficiency
Self-worth
Separation and divorce
Service

Sickness
Silence
Sin
Social concern
Solitude
Spirituality
Stillness
Strength
Stress
Success
Suffering

Thanksgiving
Time
Tolerance
Trinity
Troubled times

Trust
Truth
Unemployment
Unity

Values
Virtue
Vocation
Vulnerability

Weakness
Why?
Will of God
Wonder
Work

Youth

Index of Selected Themes

Advent and Christmas:
January 19-20; February
12-13; May 16-28;
December 24-25.

Belief: January 10-11; March
7-10; April 3; October 8;
November 4-6; December 10.

Bereavement and dying:
January 12-15; February
4, 7, 16-18, 25; March 12,
25; July 24; October 3;
December 6.

*Christian life and
sacraments:* January 5, 9,
25-31; February 1-3,
20-23; March 2-5, 28;
April 7, 9-13, 21-24; May
5-10; June 10-13, 18,
25-27; July 27, 30;
August 6-8, 10; September 29-30; October 1-2;
December 13-14.

Comforting words: February
7, 16-18; March 17-20,
22-25, 29-31; April 1-2,
4-6, 15-17; May 3-4; June
3-7, 9-10, 14, 20, 27; July
2, 5-7, 20-23; August 1,
9, 16, 19; October 4-5, 7;
November 13-14, 18;
December 3, 7-8.

Family: June 11; July 8-9;
August 5.

Holy Week and Easter:

February 15, 26; April 8;
May 1, 16, 20-22; September 27; October 5;
November 19.

Lent: February 12-13; March
16-21; April 14; June 1;
July 20-23; October
26-28.

Mary: July 10-15.

Pentecost: April 25-27.

Prayer: January 1-3; July
17-19, 25, 28-29; August
8, 21-31; September
1-13; October 6, 15;
November 7-8, 28-29.

Priesthood: July 24;
September 18-20.

Self-directed retreat:
January 2-4, 7-8, 20-24,
28; February 5; March
15; April 6, 20-21, 24;
May 17-28, 31; August
23-24, 28; September 2,
5-7; October 7, 9-13,
20-25, 31; November
1-3; December 15, 21-23,
26, 29.

*Service and concern for
others:* February 6;
March 30; May 2, 9,
13-15, 30; June 11, 15-
17, 19, 21-24, 28-30; July
1-3; August 2-3, 11, 15,
17-18, 20; September 28;

Sources and Acknowledgements

Permission to reproduce copyright material in this book is gratefully acknowledged:

'Adversity', Martin Luther King, *Strength to Love*, 'Availability', John Sayers, *The Burrswood Herald*; 'Baptism', Archbishop Oscar Romero, *The Violence of Love* (Collins/Fount, 1989); 'Bereavement', © Frances M. Brown; 'Bereavement', John Austin Baker, *The Whole Family of God* (Ward Lock/Cassell, 1981); 'Bereavement' © Eilis Ni Fheich; 'Brokenness, Love's demands, Obedience, Religion, Work Love of the World', collected papers of Canon R.E.C. Browne, ed. Canon Ian Corbett (Churchman, 1986); 'Brokenness', Jean Vanier, *The Broken Body* (DLT, 1988); 'Change' Edward E. Ford and Robert L. Zorn, *Why be lonely?*; 'Christianity', Archbishop George Carey, *I Believe* (SPCK); 'Christ-like' and 'Discipleship', Cardinal Basil Hume OSB, *Light in the Lord* (St Paul Publications, 1991); 'Church', St Bernard of Clairvaux, *Love Without Measure* (DLT); 'Companions' and 'Empathy', Alastair V. Campbell, *Rediscovering Pastoral Care* (DLT 1986); 'Compassion', Chogyam Trungpa, *The Myth of Freedom and the Way of Meditation* (Shambala, 1976); 'Confidence', Fr Alfred Delp, *Prison Meditations*; 'Confidence', W. Scott McPheat; 'Heaven', David Winter; 'Meeting God', J.I. Packer; 'Poverty', Jurgen Moltmann; 'Solitude', Henri Nouwen; 'Time', Michael Griffiths; 'Weakness', Robert Girard; 'Wonder', Rollo May quoted in *Still Waters, Deep Waters* (Hodder & Stoughton 1977); 'Conversion', © Paul Robb SJ; *Conversion as a Human Experience* (Studies in the Spirituality of Jesuits); 'Conversion', Malcolm Muggeridge, *Conversion*; 'Crucifix', © Connie Ford; 'Death', Dorothy Solle, *Die Hinreise*; 'Death', *Forms of Prayer for Jewish Worship*; 'Defeat', Roderick Strange, *The Catholic Faith* (Oxford University Press); 'Difficulties', 'Redundancy', 'Unemployment', 'Youth', from *Further Everyday Prayers*; 'Eternal life', 'Guilt', 'Prayer as gift', Henri Boulad SJ, *All is Grace* (SCM Press 1991); 'Faith', Marco Barbone in *Light from Behind the Bars* by Carmelo di Giovanni (St Paul Publications); 'Dying', Chogyam Trungpa, *The Tibetan Book of the Dead* (Shambala 1977); 'Easter', *Contemporary Prayers for Public Worship*; 'Encouragement', *Short Prayers for a Long Day*; 'End of the world', Gerald Jampolsky, *Teach Only Love*; 'Eucharist: A Prayer Inspired by the Mass', 'Love: Written in Contemplation', 'Night prayer: A Prayer Written for Evensong Intercessions', 'Trust: Written for Someone in Distress over a Loved One's Illness', © Judith Ann Pounder; 'Fallibility', 'Resurrection', Archbishop John Habgood, *Confessions of a Conservative Liberal* (SPCK); 'Farewell', George Appleton, *Journey for a Soul*; 'Forgiveness', Fr Benedict Heron OSB, *Inner Healing* (DLT) 'Forgiveness', Sir Laurens van der Post, *A Far-off Place* (Chatto & Windus); 'Future', Christopher Dawson, *Dynamics of World History*; 'Future', C.P. Cavafy, *The Complete Poems of Cavafy* (The Hogarth Press); 'Gentleness', Lord Longford, *The Life of Jesus*

Christ (Sedgwick & Jackson), 'Giving', © Fr Andrew O'Donohoe; 'God', © Juan Arias; 'God', 'Perspective', Delia Smith, *A Journey into God* (Hodder & Stoughton); 'God', St Mechthild of Magdeburg *Beguine Spirituality* (SPCK, 1989); 'God', C.S. Lewis, *The Four Loves;* 'God's action', 'Trust', Carlo Carretto, *Journey Without End* (DLT); 'God's action', Reeve Robert Brenner, *The Faith and Doubt of Holocaust Survivors;* 'Gospel', Michel Quoist, *With Open Heart* (Gill and Macmillan 1983); 'Gratitude', 'Solitude', Thomas Merton, *Thoughts in Silence* (Abbey of Our Lady of Gethsemani); 'Growth', Jean Vanier *Community and Growth* (Darton, Longman and Todd, 1991); 'Handicapped', Elizabeth Greeley, *Disabled I Trust;* 'Happiness', Edward E. Ford and Robert L. Zorn; 'Hell', Robert Raines, *Reshaping the Christian Life;* 'Holiness', Ruth Burrows, *Interior Castle Explored* (Sheed & Ward); 'Holiness', Donald Nicholl, *Holiness* (DLT 1987); 'Holiness', reproduced from *In Perspective* by Rosemary Hartill (with the permission of BBC Enterprises Limited); 'Holy Spirit', Martin H. Padovani, *Healing Wounded Emotions;* 'Hope', Bruce Milne, *The End of the World* (Kingsway Publications); 'Hope', published in the Compassionate Friends newsletter; 'Hope' and 'Loneliness', John J. McCullagh, *In the bits and pieces: random reflections on dilemmas of life* (The Columba Press); 'Humanity', Mary Kenny, *Why Christianity Works* (Michael Joseph); 'Humanity' and 'Sickness', Michael Mayne, *A Year Lost and Found* (DLT); 'Humility', Thomas Keating, *Open Mind, Open Heart;* Humility', Ruth Burrows, *The Watchful Heart;* 'Humility', William Barclay; 'Inadequacy', Cardinal Basil Hume OSB, *Searching for God* (Hodder & Stoughton); 'Integrity', Dr Tony Lake, *Living with Grief* (Sheldon Press/SPCK); 'Intercessions', John Baillie, *The Oxford Book of Prayers* (OUP); 'Jesus Christ', Richenda C. Scott, *Tradition and Experiences* (George Allen and Unwin, 1964); 'Jesus Christ', Henri Nouwen, *Circles of Love;* 'Jesus Christ', E. Shillito, *Jesus of the Scars* in J.D. Morrison (ed) Masterpieces of Religious Verse (Harper & Row, 1948) quoted in *Rediscovering Pastoral Care;* 'Jesus Christ', Martin Israel, *The Pearl of Great Price – a Journey to the kingdom* (SPCK, 1988); 'Jesus Christ's presence', Malcolm Muggeridge, *Jesus – The Man Who Lives* (Collins); 'Jesus Christ's presence', Thomas Keating, *Open Mind, Open Heart;* 'Jesus Christ's way', Richard Foster, *Freedom of Simplicity;* 'Joy', Mother Teresa of Calcutta, *In the Silence of the Heart* (SPCK, 1983); 'Lent', © Ann Lewin; 'Life', © Fleur Dorrell; 'Life', © Estate of Terence Cardinal Cooke; 'Life', Karol Wojtyla, *The Way to Christ* (Harper & Row, 1984); 'Life', R.S. Thomas, *The Bright Field;* 'Life', Archbishop George Carey; 'Life', 'Sabbath', *Forms of Prayer for Jewish Worship* (The Reform Synagogues of Great Britain, 1977); 'Listening', John Veltri SJ, *Orientations Vol. 1* (Loyola House, Ontario, Canada, 1979); 'Listening', Joan Gibson, *Living in Perspective* (Gateway Books); 'Listening', 'Prayer', 'Silence', 'Will of God', Thomas H. Green SJ, *Opening to God;* 'Love', Max

Muller, *Thoughts on Life and Religion*; 'Love', © Bishop Richard Harries; 'Love's meaning', © Jean Vanier; 'Love of God', Anthony de Mello, *The Song of the Bird*; 'Love of God', Simone Weil, *Gateway to God* (Collins Ltd); 'Love's strength', D. Adam, *The Edge of Glory* (SPCK/Triangle); 'Marriage', Hanna Ahrens, *Who'd be a Mum!*; 'Marriage anniversary', Rosemary Atkins & others, *Joined in Love* (Collins); 'Mary', © Wilfrid McGreal; 'Mary', Henri Nouwen, *Seeds of Hope* (DLT); 'Mary', © Timothy Dudley-Smith; 'Mary', Theotekno of Livia, *Sing the Joys of Mary* (St Paul Publications); 'Meaning', © Gerard W. Hughes; 'Meeting God', Rabbi Lionel Blue, *The Guide to the Here and Hereafter* (Collins, 1988); 'Mercy', Ladislaus Boros, *God is with us*; 'A Missionary's Nunc Dimittis', © James Good; 'Morning prayer', 'Night prayer', © Sister Joan; 'Offering', Karl Rahner, *Prayers for Meditation* (Burns & Oates); 'Old age', Phillippe Zeissig (Labor et Fides, 1987); 'Others', Albert Schweitzer, *Memories from Childhood and Youth*; 'Pain', C.S. Lewis, *The Problem of Pain* (Collins/Fount 1957); 'Patience', 'Self-sufficiency', 'Spirituality', Peter Marshall, *Mr Jones, Meet the Master* (Collins/Fount); 'Perspective', George Appleton, *One Hundred Personal Prayers Old and New* (Lutterworth Press 1988); 'Perspective', © Estate of Malcolm Muggeridge; 'Poverty', Metropolitan Anthony of Sourozh, *School for Prayer*; 'Poverty', Carlo Carretto, *Letters from the Desert* (DLT 1972); 'Poverty', Co-workers of Mother Teresa, *In the Silence of the Heart* (SPCK); 'Prayer', Ruth Burrows, *Guidelines to Mystical Prayer* (Sheed and Ward); 'Prayer', © Henri Nouwen; 'Prayer', Karl Rahner SJ, *Encounters with Silence* (Burns & Oates 1978); 'Pity', Christy Brown, *Background Music* (Secker & Warburg); 'Poverty', Stephen Neill, *A Genuinely Human Existence* (Doubleday, 1959); 'Prayer', Tessa Sheaf (*The Tablet*, 28 March 1992); 'Prayer and contemplation', *The Ladder of Perfection* (Penguin); 'Prayer, the practice', Tito Colliander in *Seasons of the Spirit* edited by George Every, Richard Harries and Kallistos Ware (SPCK/Triangle 1990); 'Prayer – a necessity' and 'Self-denial', James Houston, *The Transforming Friendship, A Guide to Prayer*, (Lion); 'Prayer's language', Rabbi Lionel Blue, *Day Trips to Eternity*; 'Prayer of Jesus', John Main OSB, *Moment of Christ* (DLT); 'Present Moment', Dom Bede Griffiths, *The Universal Christ: Daily Readings with Bede Griffiths* (DLT); 'Present moment', 'Time', Bishop David Hope, *Friendship with God* (Collins/ Fount); 'Priesthood', Cardinal Basil Hume OSB, *Light in the Lord* (St Paul Publications 1991); 'Priesthood', © Estate of Cardinal Terence Cooke; 'Priesthood', © John Farrell OP; 'Reality', Gerard W. Hughes, *Walk to Jerusalem* (DLT); 'Redemption', Thomas A. Marsh, *The Furrow*, April 1992; 'Reflection', Bishop John Crowley, *Prayer in a Busy Life* (CTS); 'Religious experience', Paul Tournier, *The Strong and the Weak* (SCM); 'Respect', © Jane Milward; 'Scripture', Margaret Clarkson, *Single*; 'Silence', Max Picard, *The World of Silence* (Harvill, 1952); 'Self-worth', Ronald Rolheiser OMI, *Forgotten Among the Lilies* (Hodder

& Stoughton); 'Service', Sean McDonough SSC, *The Greening of the Church* (Cassell, 1990); 'Silence', James Roose-Evans, *Inner Journey, Outer Journey* ; 'Sin', Pierre Riches, *Back to Basics*; 'Sin', Michel Quoist, *With Open Heart* (Gill and Macmillan 1983); 'Social concern', Martin Luther King, *Strive Toward Freedom*; 'Stillness', © Patricia M. Vardigans; 'Suffering', Fr Eric Doyle OFM; 'Strength', Harold S. Kushner, *When Bad Things Happen to Good People* (Pan Books, 1982); 'Suffering', H.A. Williams, *Someday I'll Find You* (Mitchell Beazley International); 'Suffering', John Dalrymple, *Costing Not less than Everything* (DLT); 'Suffering', Dom Edmund Jones OSB, *Yes, Lord, I Believe;* 'Suffering', Mary Craig, *Blessings;* 'Trinity', Fr Eric Doyle; 'Troubled times', David Adam, *Tides and Seasons: Modern Prayers in the Celtic Tradition* (SPCK); 'Trust', Michael Hollings, *I Will be There* (McCrimmon Publishing); 'Trust', Gerard W. Hughes, *God of Surprises* (DLT); 'Trust', Ruth Burrows, *The Watchful Heart*; 'Thanksgiving', Wang Mingdao, *Prayers and Thoughts of Chinese Christians* (Mowbrays, 1991); 'Vocation', David Gooding, *An Unshakable Kingdom* (Inter Varsity Press, 1989); 'Vulnerability', © Anna McKenzie; 'Why', Father Andrew, *A Gift of Light: A Collection of Thoughts from Father Andrew* (Mowbray 1968); 'Why?', © Liz Selby, *Travellers' Tales – Poetry from Hospice*, edited by Jane Eisenhauer; 'Will of God', Thomas H. Green SJ, *Darkness in the Marketplace* (Ave Maria Press); 'Will of God', Benedict Groeschel CFR, *Thy Will be Done* (Alba House); 'Will of God', Archbishop Michael Ramsey, *Gateway to God*; 'Youth', Episcopal Church, U.S.A.

Every effort has been made to ensure the accuracy of copyright acknowledgements. The compiler and publishers of this book apologise for any inadvertent omissions of copyright and will rectify this in future editions where such omissions or infringements are brought to their attention.

By the same author:

Words of Wisdom

"Words of comfort skillfully administered are the oldest therapy known to man," said George Bernard Shaw.

"Father Danny Cronin has brought together in this book an interesting collection of thoughts, one for each day. People today often find that they do not have time for reading spiritual books, others are not accustomed to the practice of spiritual reading. This book will help those who want something brief, and it may be an encouragement to others to read books that feed our faith. ... There is much in this book to feed the spirit. It is hoped that it will prompt and inspire quiet meditation and fervent prayer" (*Cardinal Basil Hume*, in the Preface).

Words of Wisdom is sure to bring inspiration and comfort to many people, most of all to those in special need – the sick, those in hospital or in prison, those recently bereaved. It is also intended for anyone who is interested in growing in the spiritual life.

ISBN 085439 284 X   £4.95

Through the year with
WORDS OF COMFORT
Fr Daniel Cronin

'The mass of men lead lives of quiet desperation', wrote H.D. Thoreau. If there is any grain of truth in those intriguing words then there must be many people who are searching for some 'words of comfort' to help them make sense of their lives.

This book, a companion volume to *Words of Wisdom*, responds to that need, by being both challenging and reassuring. It provides a well-chosen thought or quotation from the lived experience of a wide selection of authors.

This is an area where theory counts for little, but experience for everything. The authenticity of *Words of Comfort* stems from the type of people who have contributed to it – perhaps best summarised by the young doctor who learns that he is terminally ill at the age of 37 and shares his struggle to come to terms with that fact. He does so successfully by unravelling his own spirituality and finally realises that Jesus Christ is the great comforter: *'Our Lord is not standing by seeing how we get on, he is actually suffering with us... suffering allows us to identify ourselves most closely with our Lord'* (Dr J.H. Casson).

This is a book of hope, humour and inspiration which will indeed bring comfort to those who read it.

ISBN 085439 344 7   £5.95